1795

The support older people want and the services they need

This publication can be provided in alternative formats, such as large print, Braille, audiotape and on disk. Please contact: Communications Department, Joseph Rowntree Foundation, The Homestead, 40 Water End, York YO30 6WP.
Tel: 01904 615905. Email: info@jrf.org.uk

The support older people want and the services they need

Roger Clough, Jill Manthorpe, OPRSI (Bert Green, David Fox, Gwyn Raymond and Pam Wilson), Vicki Raymond, Keith Sumner, Les Bright and Jinny Hay

The **Joseph Rowntree Foundation** has supported this project as part of its programme of research and innovative development projects, which it hopes will be of value to policy makers, practitioners and service users. The facts presented and views expressed in this report are, however, those of the authors and not necessarily those of the Foundation.

Joseph Rowntree Foundation, The Homestead, 40 Water End, York YO30 6WP
Website: www.jrf.org.uk

About the authors

Roger Clough, Emeritus Professor of Social Care at Lancaster University, is the director of *Eskrigge Social Research*, focusing on research for policy and practice.

Jill Manthorpe is Professor of Social Work at King's College London and co-director of the Scoial Care Workforce Research unit.

Older People Researching Social Issues (OPRSI) is a consortium of men and women who hold a Certificate in 'Research Methods for Older People' from Lancaster University.

Vicki Raymond is a freelance trainer providing training to voluntary, educatin and busiess organisations on disability.

Keith Sumner is Acting Director – Strategic Commissioning for the *Greater Peterborough Primary Care Partnership*.

Les Bright is now an independent consultant specialising in older people's issues, and has worked for national and local organisations.

Jinny Hay is Prevention Strategy Manager in Adult Social Care services, having been a social worker and written a dissertation on preventative services.

First published 2007 by the Joseph Rowntree Foundation

ISBN 978 1 85935 539 8 (paperback)
ISBN 978 1 85935 540 4 (pdf: available at www.jrf.org.uk)

A CIP catalogue record for this report is available from the British Library.

Cover design by Adkins Design.

Prepared and printed by:
York Publishing Services Ltd, 64 Hallfield Road, Layerthorpe, York YO31 7ZQ
Tel: 01904 430033; Fax: 01904 430868; Website: www.yps-publishing.co.uk

Further copies of this report, or any other JRF publication, can be obtained either from the JRF website (www.jrf.org.uk/bookshop/) or from our distributor, York Publishing Services Ltd, at the above address.

Contents

Acknowledgements

We should like to thank the older people who participated in the focus groups, the professionals who responded to our surveys and those who attended the end-of-project consultation meeting in November 2005. Thanks are also due to the editors of the British Association of Social Workers' journal *Professional Social Work* and of *Nursing Older People* for publicising our surveys, and to the Association of Directors of Social Services for approving the survey of local authorities.

1 Unmet needs – and the services older people want

The task we were set

In 2004, the Joseph Rowntree Foundation (JRF) responded to the findings from a series of research and consultations by setting up an Inquiry into unmet needs for low-level services among older people. This was published in November 2005 (Raynes *et al.*, 2006). The Foundation also commissioned this further piece of work to comment on current practices and to distil the views of people with expertise and experiences of this subject. Our task was not to follow in well-worn tracks, doing no more than deepening existing ruts. If, at the end of our study, we came up with the conclusion that there were 'not enough low-level services', we would have achieved little. Rather we were to map the barriers and look to producing a resolution that older people would value.

The project that we discuss in this report worked in parallel with the Inquiry and both were conducted on behalf of the Independent Living Committee of the JRF. The way we have tackled our brief has developed as we have worked at the task and discussed with our research adviser, Alex O'Neill. We have tried to pursue the broad aims of the Committee, which are set out in Box 1.

Box 1 Aims of the JRF Independent Living Committee

- To identify and understand the range of diverse *barriers* to achieving person-centred support for Older People, Disabled People and Service Users.
- To identify *approaches* to address these barriers, which will have credibility with users and viability in practice.

This Committee will look at tools and approaches which people (individually and as 'movements' of older people, Black & Minority Ethnic communities, disabled people, service users) have said are valuable. It will also look at the opportunities and barriers within services to bringing more person-centred support. The focus over the three years of project funding is likely to be:

I *Looking backwards*, what has already been learned to date about barriers to choice and control, and possible solutions?

Continued overleaf

II *Looking currently*, what is happening, what are the exemplars of good practice? Where do problems still rest? What are the bridges and barriers to person-centred/user-controlled support?

III *Looking forwards*, what does this tell us about a new or reframed vision for appropriate support? Can services truly be made responsive to the needs of users or will Direct Payments be the only credible approach to choice and control in the future?
(JRF, 2005)

At an early meeting of the project's advisory group we discussed possible options, drawing on themes that were emerging within other work undertaken for the Independent Living Committee.

- It might be that, with existing resources being targeted at older people with higher support needs, there cannot any longer be a consensus that 'low-level support' can be met through public funds.
- Alternatively, it might be that (in terms of saving on 'ambulances downstream', that is reduced need for expensive crisis services, for want of earlier preventive services 'upstream') a focus solely on high support needs is inefficient in terms of *sustainability and cost-effectiveness.*
- It might be that, while the sustainability and cost-effectiveness arguments are not proven, there is a *human rights* argument to support the provision of low-level support from public funds.
- It might be that, despite eloquent argument in the above, the *reality* is that service delivery needs to work within the resources available. If so, there are questions about what can be achieved by reframing or shifting resources.

Furthermore we undertook to identify sustainable ideas of good practice. What are the exemplars of good practice and what are the policy, organisational, guidance, human or infrastructural barriers to achieving these?

The information that forms the basis of this report

The knowledge base for this report comes from a variety of sources.

1 Seven discussion/focus groups of older people across England.

2 Surveys of:
   - local authority staff in commissioning of services
   - front-line social workers
   - nurses.

3 Study of policy and research literature.

4 Early meetings with staff from Secretariat of the Inquiry.

5 Reviews by the project team and other invited experts.

The policy context

There is not space in this report to set out the recent policy initiatives that relate to the direction and performance of social care, the values that underpin guidance and the systems that are to be adopted. Many of them are summarised in the set of reports from the Audit Commission and Better Government for Older People (2004) and the National Strategy on Ageing (DWP, 2005).

Furthermore, early in 2006, as we have been putting the final touches to the report, there have been important policy initiatives stemming from Government.

- *A Sure Start to Later Life* (ODPM, 2006). The Government contends that there are parallel messages from Sure Start services for children: there should be more involvement from local communities and easier access. The aim is to combat exclusion of older people through 'comprehensive services that can empower older people and improve quality of life' (ODPM, 2006, p. 9). Notably, the document recognises that the responsibility for such developments goes far beyond social services. David Miliband, Minister of Communities and Local Government, has emphasised the importance of involving older people in communities and in supporting communities to develop solutions to the problems that confront older citizens. The overall objectives of the paper are set out:

  > First, the government's commitment to progressive, personalised services tailored to need. The second is the commitment to social justice which means services that work for all, particularly the most excluded. The third is our commitment to economically efficient services, through better prevention and joining up.
  > (ODPM, 2006, p. 9)

- The White Paper *Our Health, Our Care, Our Say* (Department of Health, 2006). This Paper, together with the earlier Green Paper *Independence, Well-being and Choice* (Department of Health, 2005a), the *National Service Framework for Long Term Conditions* (Department of Health, 2005c) and the White Paper *Choosing Health* (Department of Health, 2005b), have placed prevention high on the agenda of public authorities: they have charged both health and social care, local authorities, and voluntary and community groups, with the task of working together to achieve this. They demand more personalised services in which older people have a stronger voice. The mechanisms to achieve this in social care are through individual budgets, joint commissioning between health and social care, and an increase in care outside hospitals. They set out a vision for adult social care of services that are seamless, proactive and person centred.

We have taken these initiatives into account in reviewing the material that had been produced from our study before their publication. Welcome as the thrusts of these initiatives are, we do not think that they change the basic dilemmas that we outline in this report. We try to capture these dilemmas at the start by reporting on a number of group discussions with older people.

Asking people about the support they would like

We start this section with the conversations we held with seven groups of older people, involving 79 members, to illustrate the complexity of understanding what would help people to live more fully. The groups were of two hours' (maximum) duration, and started with an introduction covering who the facilitators were and the purpose of the project. Before the start of the workshop we had sent out details, which included the following paragraph:

> We are collecting views about the services older people need to support them in their life at home. Our focus is on the services that are often described as 'low-level' tasks such as household repairs, cleaning, shopping, gardening or the myriad aspects of living arrangements that people may not be able, or want, to do themselves. So we are trying to find out the impact of such services, which may reduce the likelihood of people having to move from their homes, on people's lives. In addition, we are looking at the systems in social services departments to assess what is known about the potential demand for such services.

We had debated at some length how to describe the project so as to avoid confining people to thinking within the current descriptions of low-level services. In the end we recognised that the necessity of saying in invitations something about the task inevitably would influence the conversations held. The problem reappeared when facilitators were starting the meetings.

It is particularly difficult to explain the meaning of the terms without giving examples, which facilitators wanted to avoid, as they did not wish to lead or direct participants.

There were great similarities in the issues, ideas and concerns that flowed from each of the groups, regardless of location, the ways in which they had been recruited or whether the facilitator made use of prepared vignettes. All the material that follows in this section comes from these discussion groups. We have divided the discussions into themes, and start with bullet points that sum up the items or activities that people felt exemplified what they were talking about. We follow these with a commentary on the essence of the discussion. The transcripts of the discussions were read by three members of the research team and the key themes were developed and explored.

Around the house and garden

- Cleaning generally and vacuuming in particular.
- Laundry.
- Minor household tasks: for example, replacing light bulbs, tacking down unruly carpets and other floor coverings, and 'odd jobs'.
- Putting out the 'wheelie bin'.
- Clearing snow.
- Safety and security: fitting smoke alarms, peep holes, additional locks to windows and gates.
- Grab rails, ramps and other aids to mobility (*not* subject to occupational therapist assessment).
- Handyperson activity: for example, dealing with ill-fitting or broken locks and catches, fences damaged by the weather.
- Garden maintenance: cutting grass, weeding flowerbeds, pruning trees.

Commentary

Some of these needs can clearly be seen as preventive or ways of minimising risk. For example: ensuring that carpets are properly secured removes one possible cause of falls; pruning overhanging trees and bushes permits more light to enter the home, contributing to a safer environment; moving a wheelie bin to the designated pick-up point, and clearing snow, were identified as physically demanding tasks that might compromise health or safety.

Older people identified these links and were bewildered that public bodies, which claimed to be taking a holistic look at people's needs, did not seem to be able to make the same linkages between risks and possible responses. For women, in particular, some household jobs were difficult in later life and some did not know of reliable and reasonably priced tradespeople. One said:

> I live alone and *[want]* somebody who could come in and, you know, do things. I can't get up on a ladder for instance, any more. So I need somebody to do these things.

Fitting grab rails strategically in bathrooms and other parts of the house also creates a safer environment, sometimes in advance of actually needing such adaptations. People cited the long waits they had been told to expect before being seen at home by an occupational therapist (OT) as a reason for getting on with the job themselves, or at least getting someone to do it for them. While many in the groups recognised that OTs could get work ordered, or advise on the equipment that might best suit their needs and where it should be placed for maximum effect, these professionals were often known to be in short supply. Frequently people had decided it was best to get on without the benefit of their advice.

Being safer as a result of attending to either minor household tasks or fitting equipment to prevent accidents was only part of the issue. Feeling safer around the house was also a product of having greater security. This was accomplished either by fitting alarms and locks or by maintaining the exterior of the house so that it did not give the appearance of being neglected or easy to enter, perhaps signalling the vulnerability of the occupant.

People reported having 'peace of mind' as a result of someone attending to these tasks for them and, in many instances, it was family help that made the difference between anxiety about such matters or otherwise. This type of help was flexible and informal. One person spoke of the difference of having your son or friend hanging a picture for you, as part of a social call, and the difficultly and complications of finding someone commercially. The commercial help had to have employment standards in place:

> It's the replacement friend *[you want]* and no friend is, no friend has had the fire officer visit to check his insurance.

We found that, in some areas, people knew of local schemes that could give some help but provision seemed uneven, such schemes' criteria were not well known and contact details were not easily obtainable.

Staying in and going out

- Getting in/out of the bath.
- Being alone.
- Feeling alone.
- Meeting and making friends.
- Feeling safe in the street/neighbourhood.
- Dearth of public conveniences.

Commentary

A number of people mentioned the problems encountered – or envisaged – in continuing to look after themselves without any other help. Getting in and out of the bath was seen by some as a big problem, which not only required them to take great care, but also restricted the number of times they considered taking a bath. Help with bathing was an activity that many considered ought to be available, sometimes just equipment that might give greater security, without them then succumbing to having help on a number of other fronts where they were still managing.

Adjusting to living alone brought on great loneliness for some people and was often an accompaniment to the enduring sadness that several felt as a result of being bereaved. People cited the importance of getting out of the house to see others, at the same time noting the difficulty of getting out because of reduced mobility or restrictions associated with transport problems, discussed further below. This then highlighted the potential importance of volunteer visiting or befriending schemes, where volunteers were matched to people who were socially isolated. These fulfilled different functions: a regular visitor who might then provide companionship; an activity; or, in some cases, someone to pick up on small routine tasks outside the older person's capacity, such as fitting a new light bulb.

Many people spoke very warmly and positively of lunch clubs and other social groups (even if they did not make use of them). Getting out of the house with a sense of purpose provided a highlight to an otherwise flat week, and was a way of extending networks of friends and acquaintances, often considered to be more important than sources of more formal help.

In terms of feeling safe on the street people mentioned the changing use of pavements – previously the preserve of pedestrians, but now used in some areas for cycling by children and adults. People with visual impairments mentioned problems with 'street furniture' and the need to take avoiding action in the face of cyclists and skateboarding children and youths. However, some older people wanted to explain that they did not always view young people or their neighbourhoods as dangerous. One person said:

> I used to be a youth worker; these young people like to hang around, they do nothing, they're not interfering, they just hang around.

The decrease in the number of public toilet facilities – free of vandalism – was mentioned as a source of anxiety too, as some people planned journeys to coincide with their need to feel comfortable and to avoid 'accidents'. In one area, the group noted that there were now no public toilets along the High Street or at the station and one person said how older people have to go 'cap in hand to pubs to ask to use their toilets', while others made use of the local McDonald's. Such feelings indicate that older people do not see 'Government' as being solely responsible, but consider that all sectors have responsibility for, essentially, adapting to an ageing society made up of increasing numbers of older consumers and older citizens who want to be able to participate in their communities.

Managing personal affairs

- Interpreting correspondence.
- Writing to utilities and others.
- Writing Christmas cards.
- Being advised/seeking advice.

- PIN numbers.
- Pets.

Commentary

Failing eyesight was just one factor affecting people's ability to understand correspondence they received. Others, who did not have any major sight problems, nevertheless talked of the need for support and help in reading, understanding and reacting to letters and bills. Computer-generated letters from utilities and councils were cited as being particularly confusing and capable of provoking anxiety. There seemed much scope for making sure that such correspondence was completed to standards of Plain English and made easy to read for older people (and others).

Where correspondence was a bill for a service rendered, or due in advance, there was even more scope for confusion and worries about where and when to make the payment, and how to avoid incurring any charges. Generally the public utilities had withdrawn from having a high street presence, instead leading people with queries to consider making a telephone call (or calls) to call centres. This added to the cost, or led people to leave their questions unasked, as they feared the automated systems they would have to negotiate. People did not feel that they wanted to bother hard-pressed local advice agencies for such minor matters.

This was clearly an area that caused some people a good deal of worry, and those who did not have a trusted friend or family member close at hand found worries mounting because of the combination of impersonal computerised billing, distant call centres and the lack of a local office or showroom to visit. These feelings were compounded for some by the programme of post office closures that has led to changes to the payment of retirement pensions, and by the receipt of non-payment and 'red' demands.

A minority worried about using their PIN, with several saying that they had no idea and had had no 'tutoring' in how to use it or keep it safe. Such worries about 'modern life' appeared to be reasons why some people kept in contact with the social groups they attended.

But not all reading and writing problems were associated with bill payment. Organising writing Christmas cards was cited as a worrying activity by a small number: completing the envelopes in legible handwriting, and maintaining an address book so as to ensure that networks and friendships were sustained was a challenge too. When this theme was explored, we found that some of the people who raised this subject helped other older people, generally much older than themselves (in their nineties) and in very poor health, and saw this as an activity for friends if possible. While computers are making such tasks easier for some, not all are yet skilled or confident to use such technology, but it seemed less a matter of disability *per se* and more a sign of general frailty.

Pets were cited as a source of pleasure and of company, but as a source of some anxiety if people thought they should talk about problems in the discussions. They described some of the responsibilities, generally foreseeable, arising from pet ownership, such as meeting the cost of vets' bills and, in the case of dogs, being able to exercise them.

Staying informed

- Finding out about benefits.
- Form filling.

Commentary

Another of the functions of lunch or social clubs, additional to providing companionship and refreshments, was being a source of information and advice. This was not a formal or explicit purpose in some settings but simply grew from people's knowledge and experience, and a willingness to share with others, an example of the mutuality on which so many clubs seemed to be founded.

The completion of forms, whether to obtain a benefit or to secure access to a service, was sometimes a sensitive activity, requiring people to detail their income and assets. For some there was an understandable wariness in revealing such intimate details to someone casually, and in the hearing of others. But this then meant that they needed to seek help from elsewhere. Voluntary organisations and community groups figured as providers of this type of information, coupled with advice to support people in making decisions.

Shopping

- Choice.

- Control.
- Collecting prescriptions.
- Christmas presents.
- Nutritional information and advice.
- Help selecting and trying on clothes.
- Hairdressing.

Commentary

Shopping was a source both of pleasure and of worry for many people. As with lunch clubs, variously described as 'being about more than a hot meal', shopping performs a number of different functions in the lives of older people (and of course for other age groups).

Shopping gave purpose and structure to lives, and also enabled people to remain independent and in control of how they lived their lives.

Being able to get to the shops was not always a problem. However, once there, finding things, being able to read small labels (unlike the large 'money-off' posters) and reaching items presented problems, to a degree. One person, for example, spoke of the way in which shopping was becoming more difficult.

> I'm partially sighted and, when I go in the shops, say it was different honeys, different teas, and I can't see which is which, and I keep troubling people. So, if someone came round, did shopping with me, it would make a lot of difference.

The return journey with a bag full of shopping stretched physical capabilities and those who used trolleys sometimes encountered difficulties getting on or off buses. Taxis were not an option for all, as their cost was often outside the weekly budget.

The changes to shopping areas that had occurred over the past few years, leading to larger supermarkets located on the fringes of towns and cities, had made it especially hard for some older shoppers who did not have access to cars or were not near public transport. Consequently, some older people found themselves restricted to smaller shops whose produce was often more expensive than that which was available at the out-of-town centres. For others, however, these centres were very accessible, sheltered and provided a 'day out'.

While some people thought that internet ordering and the associated delivery systems offered a way forward, many older people were keen to underline the weakness of such an approach. A shopping trip provided a social activity or outlet in the same way that lunch clubs offered companionship. Another person identified shopping trips as a stimulating experience where she pitted her wits against the shop to get herself the best value for money. And, for those who did not have access to the internet, ordering over the internet was not a realistic option.

Being able to carry on shopping – being in control of the budget and making the key purchasing decisions – was considered an important marker to being in control of life more generally.

However, when turning to public services and many voluntary organisations for support, it seemed that the threshold for obtaining help (eligibility criteria) was drawn in such a way that it was possible to have help with shopping only if an individual needed support in other ways. Direct Payments, where people receive money to pay for social care, may be able to respond to such needs but these too are available only for people who are eligible for social services support. Yet many who coped with all other activities of daily living could have benefited from help getting to and from their shop of choice, and some suggested that they would welcome being accompanied around the shop, receiving a limited amount of help reading or interpreting labels and offers. Shops may have a role in offering such a service, in the same way as many have responded to calls to provide help for people with physical disabilities and to counter discrimination by making major improvements to access.

Some people noted the value of receiving advice on nutrition – what's good or bad for your health, and why – as another dimension to their purchasing decisions and hoped that such help could be provided in the future as more food-related health scares seemed to be emerging. Managing the uncertainties of life seemed to be a theme for some older people in the discussions we held. It was not always clear that any level of help would lower this sense of risk, and indeed talking about the risks of current life seemed to be one uniting theme in the discussions. As noted above, people raised concerns about community safety and not knowing whom you could trust in getting help within the home.

Not all shopping difficulties related to getting to a supermarket to buy food; selecting clothing was another, if minor, cause of anxiety. Trying on an item of clothing is a natural part of the purchasing process but it was not always easy for people whose movement was in some way restricted and so respondents mentioned the value of accompanied shopping to assist in changing rooms but also in affirming that a garment fitted right, or looked right. For those with a circle of friends or kin living nearby this was evidently not a problem and this theme illustrated the ways in which some older people feared the implications of social isolation, or disability, while not necessarily having this experience. We found it difficult at times to distinguish whether some of the older people we talked to were drawing on their experiences or thinking about the difficulties they might face at some time in the future, and if circumstances changed in their social circles. 'Keeping up appearances' is for many people vital to maintaining self-esteem, and consists of wearing clothing that fits well and is well presented – topped off by regular visits to hairdressers. Unsurprisingly, women rather more than men mentioned the importance of hair care and, in some cases, their reliance on highly valued domiciliary visits from commercial (mobile) hairdressers. This 'low-level' help was something they managed, through contacts they made, and none reported feeling that social services or the public sector should have any role in this aspect of personal care.

Collecting prescriptions presented a problem for some people, as changes in the high street had also adversely affected some local chemists or pharmacists. For some, the prescription delivery service was welcome; others were not so aware of what might be available. As with much of the discussions, the need for regular prescriptions was not universal and yet many seemed to believe that this could lie ahead for themselves or their spouses.

Transport

- Cost.
- Accessibility.
- Fit with planned destinations.
- Driver performance.

Commentary

Transport impacts on the lives of older people in many ways. It featured as an impediment to participating in many other activities people wished to engage in because of the cost, accessibility, reliability or 'fit' with planned journeys. Routes criss-cross cities, towns and districts, but do not necessarily run from residential districts to areas where businesses such as supermarkets, or hospitals and clinics are sited, requiring people to make one or more changes of vehicle – not easy for someone who may have difficulty in negotiating the steps to alight or descend from the bus. When these changes are then coupled with timing and frequency of service, a relatively simple journey may become a half-day excursion.

The cost of public transport varied from place to place, with Londoners enjoying free travel, and a plethora of other subsidy systems limiting travel to certain times and services, thus restricting older people's travel plans. The decision to introduce a nationwide system of concessionary travel for older people is to be welcomed, but there are still some other areas requiring attention.

The introduction of accessible buses, with hydraulics that enabled the floor to be lowered to pavement level, which made it easier for people with mobility problems to get on and off the vehicle, was generally appreciated. However, people expressed concern that it was not always possible to know whether such buses would be plying the route they wanted to use – or whether, when they got to their destination, such a vehicle would be available for the return journey. Several reported on the difficulties caused by some drivers not taking sufficient concerns for passengers – ensuring that people were seated before moving off or braking too quickly.

Nonetheless, there now seem to be broad agreement that more accessible environments are making a difference to many older people's lives and expectations. People spoke of the exceptions, rather than the norm.

Future generations of older people will have been more used to car ownership. Stopping driving and giving up the car are important losses of independence and affect what is called 'social inclusion'. Having a car seemed to have a similar importance to older men as the symbolic importance of having clean net curtains to older women – both were a visible sign that they were managing and supported a feeling of self-confidence.

Socialising

- Staying in touch.
- Community participation.

Commentary

Playing a part in community life is not only about attending activities designed specially for older people. A number of those at the meetings mentioned the importance of carrying on with activities that had always mattered to them. This meant being able to continue to attend religious events or go to a pub or club. However, people were not convinced that they would be able to get the support or practical assistance for this; thus, it might be easier to be offered a place on an adapted minibus to be taken to a lunch club than to get out to a much loved local pub. Pub visits in the evening and services on Saturday/Sunday mornings also presented challenges because of the timings. For some, the changing nature of communities meant that they were less able to have social contact without planning and that neighbours were not so available to build up reciprocal relationships. As one person commented: 'Neighbours, they are out all day working'.

Leisure and recreation

- Adult education classes.
- Libraries.
- Swimming.

Commentary

Older people make heavy use of adult education classes and, in some areas, may make the difference between a class being financially viable or not. There was some concern that classes were timed for the evening to suit working adults without recognising the travel difficulties this created for some older people. Increased costs of classes were also recognised as potentially off-putting.

Libraries were considered to be an important part of community life. But some of those who were reliant on mobile libraries had concerns about the range and turnover of the stock available, and said that mobiles tended to represent the library service as it used to be – books and not much else. Visitors to traditional libraries had seen them develop their services in many welcome ways, including being a source of community information and an 'advice surgery' for others, such as Citizens' Advice.

Swimming retained a dedicated group of followers, although some people with mobility problems commented on the difficulties they faced in the changing rooms and in entering the water unaided. Making buildings and transport accessible is much appreciated by older people but many difficulties remain in thinking through people's use of local environments when they have limited or occasional mobility problems.

The complexity of what is wanted

One person spoke of wanting a person who would remember *him* in the midst of the provision of services:

> Well, sometimes if you have, say, an incident like a stroke, it could be the hospital who sends someone from social services round, who then, if you have a nice person, refers you to either one of their services or one of the area's voluntary groups that do help once your medical, shall we say, problems have been sorted out to a degree that you can adjust and cope with, but you need a little bit of social life, but you need also someone to remember.

In another group, the flow of the discussion captured the importance of: having reliable people working in your home; handypersons who would do odd jobs when wanted; value for money; and socialising:

> *Member 1:* Because I need an odd-job man quite often and where I can get one that probably wouldn't rip me off? And this sort of thing.
>
> *Facilitator:* So really it's, not only do you need an odd-job man, but you want one that you can trust?

Member 1: Yes that I can have in my home. I live alone and somebody who could come in and, you know, do things. I can't get up on a ladder, for instance, any more. So I need somebody to do these little things. And, if we had some sort of helpline where you could know that you could get through and you would be seen, some sort of information for these things.

Member 2: And leading on from that. A neighbour of ours recently lost her husband and needed some new washers on her tap. We didn't know until afterwards. It cost her £35 to have those washers fitted. Two little washers on a tap! So, I mean little things like that.

Member 3: *[And a friend of mine]*, although he had the care, he didn't have anyone who could just take him out occasionally for a cup of coffee or a treat somewhere. And that also became very important to him because that was the way he could assert some independence from the carer. And feel he had a life independently and he could talk about old times with, say, people like me who knew him over a long period with memories that couldn't be shared with the *[paid]* carer.

Box 2 Membership of the groups

- *Group 1:* eight people who belonged to the University of the Third Age (U3A), living in a rural area of England.
- *Group 2:* 15 members of a community centre group in the North West of *England.*
- *Group 3:* nine people who use a drop-in centre in a small town in the North of England.
- *Group 4:* eight members of a group that supports disabled people on visits to cultural events in London.
- *Group 5:* 25 people from black and minority backgrounds who meet at a local community centre in London.
- *Group 6:* nine tenants of a social housing scheme in the South West of England.
- *Group 7:* five members of an Age Concern social group in the South West of England.

Looking forward to care in old age

Levenson *et al.*'s (2005) study complements some aspects of ours, although theirs was focused on a younger group:

> … what middle aged people will require from care services that they might need in the future, as they grow older and find they are less able to look after themselves
> (Levenson *et al.*, 2005, p. 1)

The summary of their priorities and suggested improvements adds ballast to the point we have already made: older people do not start by thinking about care services although those we spoke to were aware of possible (or actual) disability or worsening health. We quote at length from one section of this report because it suggests that many of the points made by the older people we spoke to are opinions that do not arrive 'suddenly' on receipt of the pension. Such ideas, anxieties, resilience, preferences and values are commonly held.

Box 3 Priorities and suggested improvements from the 'middle aged' (Levenson *et al.*, 2005)

When participants discussed their personal priorities for improved care services in their old age, their key priorities were:

- to have services that enabled them to maximise and retain their independence;
- to be valued as individuals and not stereotyped because of their age.

Many participants stressed the value of low-level preventative services, and wanted access to cleaning and maintenance as much as – or more than – they wanted personal care. They also frequently mentioned the importance of a good GP service, with much nostalgia for the era of home visits to older people. Some wanted health and social care to be more co-ordinated, and felt that the division between these services was unhelpful from the point of view of the service user. They also wanted services to be delivered by fewer people, who were appropriately multi-skilled and trained for the purpose, within a system that was less bureaucratic and more generously funded than they perceived current services to be.

The highest priorities of many participants were issues that are not conventionally viewed as 'care' services. They saw improved transport for all,

Continued

and better leisure and educational opportunities, as essential underpinnings of effective care. Several also liked the idea of advocates to help older people obtain their entitlements.

Participants often mentioned that they wanted care service decisions to be less influenced by budgetary and organizational constraints. They wanted to see a more independent approach both when assessing people's needs, and when monitoring and inspecting services. Above all, they wanted respect for their individuality and to be in control of how they were helped to live their lives as fully as possible.

Seminar participants prioritised care service options as follows:

- services that promote or maintain independence rather than elements of care
- services such as social life and leisure to enable clients to remain intellectually active, for instance using a computer and getting out and about
- income
- service choices that could be adapted to the client's time of life and level of need.

Their overall ranking of service options was as follows:

1 regularly eating your preferred food

2 24-hour, on-call service for help and emergencies

3 a weekly or monthly visit from an odd-job person

4 basic dusting and hoovering

5 sufficient space for one's possessions

6 assistance with bathing at times selected by the client

7 access to qualified tutors or teachers for activities

8 help with heavier cleaning and maintenance tasks

9 someone to spend time with and talk to

10 a personal advocate

11 one's own sitting room as well as a bedroom

Continued overleaf

12 movement sensors to ensure safety within the home

13 daily transport to local shops

14 free access to comprehensive digital television

15 parking for visitors

16 someone to do the washing

17 access to a gym, swimming pool or hydrotherapy pool

18 someone to take them for a walk

19 weekly transport to local shops and other facilities.

When forced to prioritise, none of the participants chose the following options, which might be viewed as 'luxury items':

- breakfast in bed
- door-to-door transport
- one's own courtyard or outside space
- gardening services
- dog-walking services
- a spare room
- three menu choices at main meals.

Levenson *et al.* (2005, pp. 39–40)

Reflection

We have drawn from our own study and that by Levenson *et al.* (2005) to highlight both the ordinariness of much that is wanted and the difficulties in trying to meet this. What sort of person will be able, on behalf of another, to write cards and help manage correspondence, take a dog to the vet, mend a leaking tap or negotiate with a gas company? Of course it is clear that, properly, this often is or could be a relative or friend when an older person is no longer able to manage such tasks themselves. Yet the problem remains. There is repeated evidence that some older people have considerable anxieties about managing parts of their lives. Such anxieties are often not recognised by, or fall outside the scope of, current services. Even if they are short-lived problems, there is little temporary support available for such needs. And, while family care is there for many people, for many others it is distant and, for some, it is no longer available.

There can be no doubt that frequently what people want does not fall into the current boxes of service provision. The massive increase in home ownership, as evident in the older people we talked to who spoke, not of being tenants, but of the problems (and advantages) of owning your home, underpinned some of the uncertainties about what would happen if they were no longer able to do the house maintenance that home ownership necessitated. These challenges particularly preyed on the minds of some older people who felt less physically able to carry out the work or felt informal support that routinely would help with such tasks was ebbing away. As we shall discuss later, older people often have little idea of what they are entitled to, which is not surprising when there is no coherent picture of entitlement.

This point leads to some of the other issues discussed by the older people who participated in this research. They recognised that there are critical other dimensions to defining and meeting needs. Resources are not limitless; in some way society has to determine what money is available and to whom it is to be made available. They wanted the researchers to pass on the message that many older people feel that old age does not, and should not, take away the responsibility of individuals to manage within the constraints of the resources available to them. Examples such as mending leaking taps, hanging a picture and changing light bulbs highlight areas that have been the responsibility of a householder up to later life or when physical capacity is compromised. Trying to decide when others should be involved in management of such tasks is reminiscent of earlier fruitless debates as to whether a bath was designated a 'social' or a 'medical' bath. There are persuasive arguments set out earlier in this chapter for people with disabilities to be helped to go out to a favourite pub or to have assistance with clearing snow. For some, these needs are currently being met by greater use of technology or mobility aids and these will possibly become more widely available. Yet, in old age as at any other time, we will all have to make compromises. When is there a legitimate demand to be made on the State?

Certain themes stand out from the discussions held with the wide variety of older people we spoke to as being important in the way that decisions are taken about the amount of resources available, for whom they should be available and the systems that should be in place to deliver services.

1 Older people stressed that they are individuals, with different histories, different hopes and dreams, and different priorities in the management of their lives.

2 People from black and minority ethnic groups equally want access to individualised services, as above, but may have particular needs, for example for interpretation, sharing experiences in community centres or information. Other people share some of these possible access problems but in different ways, for example, those who have disabilities such as deafness or visual impairment.

3 Older people want to be involved in debating the level of resources to be made available and the ways in which resources are to be allocated. They do not share the same views.

4 Meeting the needs of older people, whether by relatives, friends, volunteers or paid staff, must be grounded in local communities. Planning at community level must find ways to deal with the realities of people's lives however they cross service or organisational boundaries.

There is a further important linguistic and conceptual point. 'Preventive' services may be referred to as 'low-level' services. Godfrey (2001), in her paper on conceptualising prevention, sought to draw on the different levels of prevention from the health literature (primary, secondary and tertiary) and root them within a socio-cultural theory of ageing. Preventive services then could be viewed as part of the resource armoury to be drawn on to support or facilitate the processes of compensation and optimisation in managing ageing. At the tertiary level, it might be managing the limitations in physical or other abilities (that could take varied forms – not only providing personal care, but also assisting people in developing their own strategies, including assistive devices, rehabilitation programmes). At the secondary level, it could be about services programmes to deal with bereavement, supporting informal caring relationships, optimising residual abilities. At the primary level, it could be about opportunities for social contact and relationships to expand social networks. Programmes/support at these different levels could be focused on individuals or on groups – through service-based or locality-based provision.

Godfrey (2006) argues that the value of the approach is that it directs attention to different levels of prevention as well as their interconnections:

> We know from the research evidence that there is an inter-relationship between physical disability and restriction, loss of social relationships, depression – which together exacerbate functional decline. So services/ support that focus on more than one aspect of need are likely to be more effective.

Getting access to services

Given the importance of the Department of Health's (2002) guidance, *Fair Access to Care Services*, to thinking about unmet need, and because it seems largely unknown to older people and those working outside social services, we set out the details below.

Box 4 ***Fair Access to Care Services***

Councils should assess an individual's presenting needs, and prioritise their eligible needs, according to the risks to their independence in both the short and longer term were help not to be provided. Councils should make changes in their practice to take a longer-term preventative view of individuals' needs and circumstances. With regard to their resources and other local factors, councils should focus help on those in greatest immediate or longer-term need ...

The eligibility framework is graded into four bands, which describe the seriousness of the risk to independence or other consequences if needs are not addressed. The four bands are as follows:

Critical – when

- life is, or will be, threatened; and/or
- significant health problems have developed or will develop; and/or
- there is, or will be, little or no choice and control over vital aspects of the immediate environment; and/or
- serious abuse or neglect has occurred or will occur; and/or
- there is, or will be, an inability to carry out vital personal care or domestic routines; and/or
- vital involvement in work, education or learning cannot or will not be sustained; and/or
- vital social support systems and relationships cannot or will not be sustained; and/or
- vital family and other social roles and responsibilities cannot or will not be undertaken.

Substantial – when

- there is, or will be, only partial choice and control over the immediate environment; and/or
- abuse or neglect has occurred or will occur; and/or
- there is, or will be, an inability to carry out the majority of personal care or domestic routines; and/or

Continued overleaf

- involvement in many aspects of work, education or learning cannot or will not be sustained; and/or
- the majority of social support systems and relationships cannot or will not be sustained; and/or
- the majority of family and other social roles and responsibilities cannot or will not be undertaken.

Moderate – when

- there is, or will be, an inability to carry out several personal care or domestic routines; and/or
- involvement in several aspects of work, education or learning cannot or will not be sustained; and/or
- several social support systems and relationships cannot or will not be sustained; and/or
- several family and other social roles and responsibilities cannot or will not be undertaken.

Low – when

- there is, or will be, an inability to carry out one or two personal care or domestic routines; and/or
- involvement in one or two aspects of work, education or learning cannot or will not be sustained; and/or
- one or two social support systems and relationships cannot or will not be sustained; and/or
- one or two family and other social roles and responsibilities cannot or will not be undertaken.

The guidance states that, in constructing and using their eligibility criteria, and also in determining eligibility for individuals, councils are expected to prioritise needs that have *immediate and longer-term critical consequences* for independence ahead of needs with *substantial consequences*. Similarly, needs that have substantial consequences should be placed before needs with moderate consequences; and so on.

There is some evidence that the new systems of giving fair access to care have pushed up the thresholds for services to very high levels. In other words, fairness may be more apparent but it is not fair that so many people do not qualify for support. Specifications such as these are important not only because they promote transparency but also because they highlight the complexities inherent in such an exercise. Godfrey (2006) comments:

> Given that support for caregivers is a key national policy objective in sustaining older people in their own homes, why are such services regarded as 'low level' support? How can Home from Hospital be similarly regarded given that this kind of support is viewed as a major component of transitional care to facilitate a resumption of independent living for older people leaving hospital?

Strange as it may seem, a further complexity arises from the uncertainty of some staff as to the purpose of assessment. Is it to work out with someone what are the areas of difficulties and what are the sorts of support that they need? Or is it the gateway to the provision of services, paid for in whole or part by the State? Thus, many authorities will have clear guidelines as to the sorts of circumstances in which an assessment is to be carried out. *Fair Access to Care Services* (Department of Health, 2002) states that anyone who appears eligible for community care services is entitled to an assessment of their needs, but this may mean other people do not have their needs examined or addressed.

In her study of one local authority, Hay (2004) identifies varied practice in relation to advice, screening and reception, summarised in Box 5.

Box 5 Enquiry, reception and screening

When reception staff judge that their social services department is not required to undertake an assessment they mainly offer information to the enquirer in the form of a phone number, leaflet or website address. Sometimes, with permission, they directly phone another agency.

When staff provide such information this is recorded on the departmental database as 'No Further Action (NFA) – Advice and Information given'. There is no follow-up of whether the person has managed to access the service and no record of outcomes for later reviews.

Continued overleaf

> We always try to go that extra mile but there again we are being squeezed because we only have so many staff … But you can't do everything and you have to make a judgement there and then, which is the most important.

Certain inconsistencies between teams are evident. One social worker said:

> I was told that they don't do cleaning and they don't do shopping and things like that. So when I came to do this job and I was told you can do shopping and you do cleaning, I was thinking, right, this is something I am not really used to.

Other practitioners in the same team did refer people into preventative services, as they found this was better for the service user in terms of choice and control, was less intrusive in revealing their financial circumstances and was kinder to their pockets:

> If you go out and all they need maybe is a bit of shopping and a little bit of cleaning then you could divert them to Age Concern.

In terms of a needs-led or a service-led approach to assessment and the consistent application of *Fair Access to Care Services* (FACS), for some practitioners, the focus was again on those service users deemed to be at a level of higher risk:

> If you are asking, do we go out and do some totally objective assessment completely free of any kind of decisions and then kind of match services to the assessment after, then no, we don't … we concentrate our energies on the risks and if we deal with anything other than the highest risks then it's in a very inconsistent and *ad hoc* way …

> We tend to go by what our own teams will do … The Y area, they are forever refusing to take any day care whatsoever unless it's because of the carer. They say 'No, we don't provide that service' but that's not true – we do provide that service.

> When we first started I think we were encouraged to literally screen people out. I think there has been a turnaround and I think teams are more accepting of things now, but certain areas are not.

Continued

> I think the nature of the contact has changed as well, because you don't get the face to face with people ... it can be harder over the telephone because you haven't got somebody's face to actually pick up on what they're not saying. You have to learn to probe on the telephone. And I think we are all quite good at that ...
>
> Often they say they're coping, they don't have any problems but when you probe a little bit deeper, you say 'Well how are you doing that?', then often they're doing things which in certain ways are very dangerous.

Hay highlights the problem-focused approach of staff:

> We ask about their daily living tasks. Whether they're independent on getting up. Whether they can do their meals. What benefits they receive. Is anyone helping them with shopping? How do they do all that?

Some staff did go beyond the practical:

> If they were particularly isolated, then I know it sounds like a low priority, but we still pass them on if they want to go somewhere ... I should think there's an awful lot of elderly people out there who are isolated but are able to cope with their own personal care that don't get in touch with us so, they're not being identified.
> (Hay, 2004, pp. 47–53)

Key themes and the structure of this report

There is a strongly held view that, in spite of rhetoric, older people do not get the services that they want. We have explored what people would like, trying to get a hold of the realities of daily living and the support that people say they need. Much of the material on which we draw comes from surveys, questionnaires and group discussions – traditional tools of research. Alongside this we incorporate evidence from research studies. However, there is one further dimension that is less common in reports of this kind. Collectively, members of the research team have been steeped in the field of social care for a total of over 200 years. In our analysis we draw on this experience. In addition, during the life of the project, members of the team have had their own contacts with social care services, often for family members. Inevitably, we have reflected on these experiences alongside the reflections on the project. It would be naive to ignore the impact they have had on our work. It is for this reason that we have chosen to follow this chapter with anonymised stories from research team members. They show the difficulties in trying to get advice and help, covering what might seem a straightforward approach to get a hearing test and hearing aids, and the far more complicated situations in which older people begin to find that they are not coping as well as they had been.

There are two important points about the way in which these stories fit into the report as a whole. The first is that they highlight the complexity of language. We started with the terminology of the project: 'unmet needs for low-level services'. But who decides what is a need? The term 'low-level' was created to describe a service that did not demand high technical skill. Yet, it seems to suggest that a service is less important than one that would be categorised as high-level. As the examples show, people may simply want a service for moderate hearing loss or they may want the house cleaned alongside intensive personal care.

Second, as, sadly, is common to many accounts, they illustrate the complexities and problems of negotiating with social and health services. We pick up on both of these points in the final chapters, presenting material about successful services that help people better manage their lives.

In Chapter 3 we look at the responsibilities of State and citizens. One of the uncertainties that now exist for older people is that of knowing what they can or should expect from the State. The NHS was understood to provide care that was free at the point of delivery from cradle to grave. Given more demands for treatment and care, higher expectations with more choice, a growth of private treatment and alternative medicine, that assumption no longer holds. 'Social care', a phrase that would not have been used in the 1940s, in any case has always been more vague in the sense of what it comprises and what is the equivalent of 'not being well enough and so going to see the doctor'? With larger disposable incomes, more people have taken the option that was always available to those with more money, the hiring of people to do work to look after you and your home, or the purchase of equipment to do much of this work. Today, we argue, there is no clarity as to what the State should provide in the field of social care.

In Chapter 4 we turn to consider social services departments' practice, largely from the perspective of managers and practitioners. Material from our surveys is incorporated here. We note the dilemmas posed to social services departments on behalf of society in trying to meet the needs for personal care, often to very high levels, alongside the needs for the sorts of services we have been describing, the writing of Christmas cards, the moving of a wheelie bin, or the development of a transport system that lets people get to the events they want to get to. What gets in the way of such provision? What examples are there of good practice?

In the final chapter we re-examine some of the key themes, looking for resolution.

2 Wanting help: older people's stories

Scenario 1: Managing hearing loss

Mr Cloke, in his sixties, had had a hearing test with the NHS five years previously and was assessed as having mild to moderate hearing loss. At that stage he decided not to have hearing aids. When his hearing got worse his GP processed the request for another test, but:

- the waiting list was to be at least eight months
- pursuing options under 'patient choice' produced nothing suitable to speed up the process
- private options were examined: assessing the quality of providers and systems was very difficult even using organisations such as RNID and the Hearing Aid Council; no impartial reviews of hearing aids could be found; costs varied by over a thousand pounds for the same equipment.

Discussion points

- Relying on 'being a good consumer' to chart your way through obtaining a service can be like working your way through a minefield.
- People want advice – and want to be assured of the quality of the advice; this was very hard to find and there was no way of knowing whether an audiologist made more money from the sale of one aid rather than another.
- 'Being a good consumer' takes time and energy.
- It is impossible to compare the quality of an NHS hearing aid with that available privately.
- Charges vary hugely, sometimes by thousands of pounds.
- 'Going private' is not hassle free.

- There is an internal question of what individuals think they *are prepared* to pay for privately, as well as what they think they *should* pay for privately. The bounds of an old welfare certainty of the same treatment for all have gone.
- While this example is from the health services, should any assistance have been available from the local council?

Scenario 2: What help? From where?

Mr Peters, a man in his early nineties, profoundly deaf, is living alone, following the death of his wife eight years previously. He has a hearing dog. He is fit and walks daily with the dog, though with increasing difficulty.

Contact 1

His son, living 300 miles away, is concerned about the steepness of the stairs in his father's house and the lack of an adequate stair rail. He phones the local social services department to ask advice. Details are taken and he is advised that there will be a long delay before a visit can be made and that his father should sleep downstairs. Three weeks later, a home visit is made and a new rail is fitted the same day with no charge being made. Mr Peters is astonished, and pleased.

Contact 2 – three years later

Mr Peters' main social contact (and occasional support for sorting out matters like a broken vacuum cleaner) is his son-in-law, who is planning to move away. (His daughter had died some years earlier.) The son-in-law is concerned that his father-in-law is becoming frailer and wonders whether he should consider a move to a residential home. Mr Peters does not want this. The GP suggests he should think about home care. First attempts to pursue that fall flat for reasons that are not clear, but seemingly because his needs are not seen to be urgent. His son tries to review with him and local services what should happen.

There are several strands to what happens.

- It is very difficult to get through to the social services department.

- The social services department wants to assess over the phone in terms of whether or not it *has* to take action. (Is he at risk in daily living? Is there an emergency? Will the current arrangements break down in the near future if nothing happens?)

- A list of home care agencies is supplied with no recommendations.

- Age Concern staff, one of the agencies, when approached say that they are not taking on new work because they cannot get the staff.

- Eventually, contact with a neighbour leads to a recommendation for a particular home care agency.

- The agency is approached; the organiser undertakes a visit (an assessment) and agreement is reached for two visits per week of one hour, primarily for cleaning and ironing; the cost is £11.40 per hour.

Immediately, this scenario illustrates the complexity of the problem.

- Should the solutions be sought privately or through the health and social care system? (It had not proved possible to find local domestic help and there were concerns about how to be sure of the quality.)

- Is there anyone available to help an individual think about their current lifestyle, future problems and the options?

- Does anyone locally know the range of different services that are available?

- Should the State have any responsibility for helping people think through their problems (whether called an 'assessment' or not)?

- Who is to pay?

- Should there be a link between primary care and access to other services? (In this scenario should a worker in one service have taken on the GP's suggestion that the person should have home care?)

- How are social services departments and primary care teams to manage demand for services, required as they are to deal urgently with anyone where there is a high risk *but also* to help in the development of what are termed 'low-level' services?

The account above was written in September 2004. In January 2005 there were changes.

Scenario 2b: What next?

Mr Peters had a stroke and was admitted to hospital. His son travelled down to the hospital the next day, arriving early afternoon to be greeted with a question from the nursing staff: 'Have you brought his clothes? The doctor says he can go home.' When the son asked whether they knew about his home circumstances and had assessed his capacity to cope at home, there was an immediate retraction. Social services staff at the hospital were unavailable but Mr Peters could stay in hospital until he was assessed. Later that week a social worker assessed him as being eligible for a place in an intermediate care scheme, where he went for two weeks. The social worker was very helpful, efficient and responsive, calling at short notice, liaising with both Mr Peters and his son. Mr Peters enjoyed his stay at the intermediate care centre, recovered well and seemed to enjoy being looked after. He surprised everyone at the case conference to plan the arrangements for his return home by saying that he wanted to stay on, had only been there for two weeks and the brochure said that people stayed for four weeks. It was pointed out to him that the brochure statement was 'up to four weeks' and that people thought he had recovered well and was ready to go home, though he should not drive again in the near future until he was reassessed as being fit. He returned home with a package of services: meals-on-wheels daily with the possibility of increased home care hours; he was to attend the intermediate care centre once a week; a taxi was arranged to take him shopping each week; Age Concern was to be asked to help him with managing his finances – though, to the surprise of the social worker, Age Concern staff said that they did not do this sort of regular assistance though would help in claims for benefits. Within days the arrangements for services at home broke down, because Mr Peters did not want the meals, the taxi service or to go to the intermediate care centre. He became ill and did not eat. The situation collapsed, perhaps because he no longer wanted the responsibility of looking after himself and his house. Mr Peters has moved to a care home and enjoys living there.

Two points are worth noting. The first is that Mr Peters had been leading a highly independent life before his stroke, including daily walks with his dog, driving and doing his own shopping. He had made it clear that he did not want to move from his house. Second, the social worker, when the link had been made after the son had challenged Mr Peters leaving hospital after 24 hours, was extremely helpful, taking on the responsibility of finding out things, passing on information and being willing to adjust her schedule to help sort things out. It was surprising that she was not aware of the services of the voluntary sector but she proved to be a very important resource for father and son. This type of help seemed only to be available because he was taking up a hospital bed or was on the threshold of residential care.

Scenario 3: Problems in getting help

Edward and May Smith are both 85, married for 59 years. Six years ago, May had a serious stroke and was in hospital for several weeks. She was extremely confused, lost the use of her left side and became blind in her left eye. During May's rehabilitation Edward's total focus was on his wife's recovery. This marked for him the beginning of a depressive illness/anxiety state, which was diagnosed three years later as the early signs of Alzheimer's disease.

At this time, no assessment was offered to either Edward or May by hospital staff. No referral to social services was made. They took it for granted that Edward would cope with his wife at home. Although May made a good recovery from the stroke, she was left with permanent blindness in her left eye and some degree of memory loss; spondylitis was also developing in her spine, making walking difficult. She needed support with dressing and washing, which Edward gladly provided.

Family members started to explore the possibility of help with housework. The local social services department stated emphatically that it did not 'do housework' and suggested contacting Age Concern. Edward and May were not convinced that they needed this help. They felt insulted by the insinuations that their house was 'dirty' and saw this as an admission of not coping and feared the deterioration that this signalled. They were unhappy about paying the prices charged by Age Concern (then £8 an hour).

The Community Mental Health Team's (CMHT's) occupational therapist (OT) then became involved with Edward, who had been referred by the GP, and embarked on stress management techniques. Her focus was on medical treatment and little was given in the way of other practical support.

At this point Edward and May conceded that they did indeed need help with housework and approached a neighbour's home help who agreed to work for three hours a week. They had also organised a gardener.

As time went on, both Edward and May became increasingly physically frail and experienced a number of falls that were medically treated as individual episodes.

Then, last year, May also started to experience a series of nose bleeds that failed to stop and on one such occasion was admitted to hospital.

One of their daughters, a social services manager in another authority, travelled to see her parents and to ascertain what help was needed.

- Hospital staff seemed totally unaware that Edward had his own problems or of any of the home circumstances.

- The daughter argued for a community care assessment both as individuals in their own right and as carers for each other.

- The OT from the CMHT, apparently, was unable to undertake this assessment.

- The social work department in the hospital refused to take a referral from the daughter – they could accept a referral only from the ward.

- Hospital staff queried the purpose of the assessment and May minimised the difficulties at home in order to be discharged to be reunited with Edward.

- She was discharged that day with no assessment but readmitted late that night following another massive nose bleed.

- She was admitted to intensive care following surgery.

Meanwhile the daughter returned home to her father who, having become increasingly frail, required support with personal care including bathing. A phone call to CMHT evoked an emergency assessment by the social worker and a care package that consisted of home care twice a day to help with washing/showering, supervision of medication and meals on wheels was established to support Edward.

May, again, was discharged without the hospital staff checking that adequate support was in place. There followed a number of events in which problems of two individuals were compounded in interaction with each other.

- The daughter tried to negotiate some support, explaining her mother's reluctance to have any help, which remained the position when social services staff contacted her.

- The daughter arranged a care alarm.

- May agreed to have home care but not day care.

- The care package for Edward supported May, as basic tasks were undertaken.
- Both Edward and May became focused on their medical conditions, and had depressive thoughts.
- May had day surgery for cataracts.
- Edward was admitted to hospital, having become very weak. He stayed there for six weeks before moving to intermediate care.
- May lost the home care services, as they had been scheduled for Edward – a problem compounded by the illness for several weeks of her private cleaner.
- Edward was discharged home. No arrangements were made for a suitable chair – his daughter arranged this; he was no longer continent and wore pads; he fell frequently; he was admitted to a care home when May went into hospital following a stroke; he returned home when she came home from hospital, but had to go back to the care home the following day after another fall.

May was struggling to manage with no care package and could not be bothered to cook. A different social worker did try to ensure that May's needs as an individual were taken into account, leading to day care and a visit from a befriender.

While this story says a lot about current services, and stories such as these may explain why the older people we talked to had generally low expectations, we focus on what it reveals about the importance of not seeing people as having low-level or high-level needs. Many of this couple's needs were low level, in the way that that term has been used. Many of the matters that really taxed the family were these 'low-level needs'. May, for example, had many 'low-level' needs, as well as those for personal and home care:

- finances (inability to handle money, write cheques, pay bills, deal with bank account, file papers)
- home maintenance (repairs, painting)
- daily living (putting out the dustbin, changing light bulbs, buying and repairing clothes)
- housework other than basic cleaning (cleaning oven, fridge and freezer).

The list of household tasks to be considered is, seemingly, endless. Other low-level support serves several functions; transport is needed not only to maintain relationships but also to get to the dentist or chiropodist.

Some of the tasks can be undertaken by existing support services. The local Care and Repair agency had been asked to assess the damp walls in the bedroom and the uneven path that could lead so easily to another fall. Others do not have any presenting solution apart from the capacity of relatives to undertake them.

Eventually both Edward and May received their full benefits entitlements – no mean feat given the complexity of government departments. Edward no longer has the capacity to be interested and May does not have regular support to help her to spend it.

Issues raised

The accounts in this chapter confirm what many studies and policy deliberations have shown.

- The focus was on high-level needs – in general, the smaller things that support people to remain at home were ignored, as were social interactions and relationships until relatively recently. Staff in statutory agencies made implicit assumptions about who was or was not 'in need of help'. As Godfrey (2006) points out:

  > This is another way in which the practices of the agency and of staff constrain what is 'eligible' need. This links up with another point made later in this report – that to be eligible for an assessment, you will have to have 'eligible service' needs. So the problem of 'unmet need' cannot only be located in the context of a 'user-centred' approach to assessment.

- There were huge difficulties in accessing appropriate help, advice and guidance, as well as accessing low-level services through the social services department, although this is where people turned in expectation of help.

- There are real difficulties in negotiating one's way through the system, in part as a consequence of the purchaser–provider split. We quote again from Godfrey (2006):

Thus, for many services – whether these be for assistive devices, help in the home or long term residential care – it is down to individuals to make the decision about what is 'right' and 'appropriate' from lists provided by social services. And where many voluntary agencies are also services providers it is difficult to see how they could also be impartial advocates in helping people come to a decision about what service might be best for them.

- It was difficult to find and negotiate with reliable trade services, such as plumbers and decorators.

- May and Edward were dealt with as two individuals, by two different teams, who produced two care packages, and seemed unable to recognise the interconnectedness of the support that one person provided for another. May was a carer and in need of services in her own right.

It remains uncertain whether the problems highlighted here will be solved in the future via individual budgets. These may be a way to link up support from social care and adaptations and other funding streams for people in similar circumstances to Edward and May. Under these schemes, which started as pilots in 2006 in 13 local authority areas in England, people who are eligible for social care services and some other services, such as a Disabled Facilities Grant, will be offered an amount of money to buy their own package of support. Yet we need to remember that new systems on their own rarely solve the complex problems outlined here.

3 The welfare mix: the responsibilities of State and citizens

People are not sure of what they can, or should, expect from the State when, in later life, they find some aspects of their life difficult to manage. They do not have a feel of the nature of the implicit contract between State and citizen. At one stage in our deliberations we called this 'the welfare agreement', a term that for us has an honourable tradition captured in the hopes expected from the 'Welfare State'. After all, welfare means 'doing well'. We have come to see that, for many, the term has become caught up with 'welfare dependency' and we think discussions need to be conducted as to the expectations of citizens in later life.

The uncertainty exists, not only for older people themselves, but also for those who commission and provide services, including front-line workers.

This is not the place for a detailed review of what older people had come to expect in terms of the support that was to be available after 1948, and there is no doubt that some see a spurious clarity in the past, with nostalgia for a command and control public sector based on wartime necessities. However, it does seem accurate that people *thought* that they understood more clearly what was available, what they could expect and who was to provide services. Of course, there are massive differences from 1948, not least in terms of the numbers of older people (those over 65, especially those over 85 years), of women who have been at work and have achieved greater independence, of people in later life who are from black and minority ethnic communities, of people who are able to be more open about their sexuality and of those who live independently with high levels of disability. Older people are also far less likely to live near their adult children.

In trying to capture briefly elements of the debate about entitlement, it is easy to forget that home care – in contrast to NHS care – with the exception of a few local authorities for a comparatively short period, has not been provided free at the point of delivery. Godfrey (2006) comments on this:

> So there is a very different framework around individual responsibility – and choice – in respect of health and social care. At the same time the boundaries around what is free at the point of use and what is not have shifted as the definitions of health and social care have shifted – but in different directions. Thus, the distinction between the 'medical' and 'social' bath was as much about redrawing the boundary of what was free at the point of use as it was about which professional/agency was responsible for

providing it. On the other hand, the development of intermediate care has meant that all transitional services within a delimited time period are free at the point of use – whoever provides them.

Yet, it remains fair to say that there is a perception that it was easier in the past to understand what was available. Significant elements of change include the following.

- A move to provide services for people in the most homelike setting, running on a continuum from a person's current home, to specialist housing, to care home, nursing home and hospital. (There have been repeated debates as to whether this move was driven by a wish to provide the best service or to cut costs.)

- Deliberate targeting of services to people in greatest need, with the former home help service becoming known as 'home care', and, more recently, services such as cleaning (that is the low-intensity services) not being provided through local authority social services departments.

- Boundary disputes between health and what is now termed social care have been rife. These have been fought over different territory but the underlying themes have remained remarkably similar. Are health or local authority staff to provide the service, with a recognition by all parties that, if the service came from the NHS, it was free to the service user and, if from social services, chargeable to the individual?

- Until the 1990s, health and social care services were provided largely by public sector staff. This has been changed as the result of a belief that competition would drive down costs, break down a presumed monopoly of the State and lead to increased efficiency, with more choice for the individual.

- Individuals choose far more than previously to purchase services. There are several reasons for this: to obtain help more quickly; to get what is presumed to be a better quality of service than that available from the State; to allow the person wanting the service to exercise both choice and control; and because many older people are more likely to be able to afford this. Direct Payments have been introduced to help people get what they want and to remain in charge of the negotiations with a worker, rather than to be seen as the recipient of care.

In setting the scene in which we portray people's uncertainties about the help to which they are entitled, there are real dangers of ignoring the context of service provision. Entitlements exist in the framework of current levels of pensions and benefits. Godfrey (2006) asks whether the debate should be set in these wider terms:

> Is it possible to talk about the responsibility of the state in relation to facets of well-being without acknowledging the deep inequalities in older age – carried over from previous life stages – and likely to exacerbate in the future with differential access to occupational pensions? For some older people, there is no 'choice' to purchase services; but for others there clearly is a choice.

The uncertainties

People's uncertainties relate to what is available, to what they are entitled to expect and to how they should behave. Many, nurtured on ideas of equality in the post-1948 era, thought it wrong to seek favoured treatment for you or yours by purchasing services. Of course lots of people might still negotiate within the bounds of their beliefs to get the best service, for example moving house to ensure access to a better school. We list the sorts of questions in people's minds.

- *What is to be provided?* Should older people pay for tasks for which formerly they had responsibility (for example, leaking taps)? What are the services or funds for which the Government (at national or local council level) should have some responsibility?
- *By whom?* How do the responsibilities of individuals, families, communities (including voluntary organisations) and the Government, at local and national level, mesh? What should be the role of the social services department (or more widely the local council) in influencing local provision? Should individuals pay (in whole or part) for chiropody, hearing aids ...?
- *How are services to be provided?* What systems?
- *How financed?* Are low-level services to be financed through the public purse? Should there be an equivalent of a 'minimum income guarantee' in the form of a 'minimum lifestyle guarantee'?
- *When should the State intervene and why?*

The facilitators of the seven groups held in the course of this study thought that people's expectations, though at times high, were not unreasonable. Some said that, as pensioners, their finances were better than they had ever known. However, others had fallen into the poverty trap of having slightly too much and therefore not qualifying for some benefits.

One theme that emerged was about the process by which people chose to pay for services. We reported earlier that some people face dilemmas of whether they *ought* to pay for services. For many the decisions were far more pragmatic. Some recounted the long waits they had been told to expect before being seen at home by an occupational therapist (OT) as a reason for getting on with a job themselves, or at least getting someone to do it for them.

Another member of a group reported how she had set about getting help at home from a private agency:

> I had an accident five years ago and I needed someone to help me do my housework. And I found someone privately and just paid her and I still have her. And that's the situation. I didn't bother to go through any system because I didn't know anything existed. I just needed someone to help me with my housework so I went and got myself paid-for help.

Like many others, she simply did not know that there might be support available or thought it was not worth the trouble.

There was discussion in groups as to which people could be relied on for help. Could (perhaps should) you rely on neighbours or family (see Box 6)?

Box 6 Should family help?

Group member 1. You can have very ... good neighbours, but you really shouldn't expect them.

Group member 2: Going into the caring situation, you don't know what's available and my father didn't want anything to do with social services ... so I was looking after him for ten years. Yes, the doctor was supplying all the medication, he came about every two years. Never saw a health visitor, well very rarely.

Facilitator: So who should have provided?

Group member 2: I don't know, because you don't know where to go, and you just plod on from day to day.

Continued overleaf

Facilitator:	Right, look at something which follows on from that ... is it up to the family to sort things out?
Group member 3:	If your family's grown up, they have their own problems.
Group member 4:	Yes.
Group member 2:	You can't make slaves out of your family.
Group member 1:	They have their own problems, they could be far away.

'And what about costs?' the facilitator asked in another group. 'Do you think the family should pay?' Members could not work out any rationale as to who should pay. They argued that whether the family should take any responsibility depended on the numbers of children, their ages and their resources.

However one member was outraged that a blind person had to pay for 'that audio-visual thing in the theatres':

> The lady's blind, I take her and she was charged £15 extra on top of the ticket. That is discrimination. If you go on a train and somebody has to meet you, you don't charge them more. So £15 is not a minor sum and ... she's blind and she needs that. It's important for her. They shouldn't. The theatre shouldn't charge £15. It's wrong.

Surprisingly, one person was told that she could not find out how much she would have to pay before a home care service started and that the hours worked could not be changed:

> The chap who did come away from his desk to give me this assessment said that's because we're so litigious these days ... The council are now very, very wary of giving any advance information ... So I didn't know what it was going to cost but I just guessed that I'd need an hour in the morning and the evening, helping with showering and that sort of thing. And as it turned out I needed much less. But it seemed I wasn't able to change from an hour down to half an hour or even a quarter of an hour would have been sufficient. The carer said, 'No I'm booked for an hour' and had to stay an hour. But I didn't know what the hour was costing anyway.

Surveys of front-line staff

We wanted to find out if the views of older people were shared by those working with them. We also wanted to know what they do at the moment if they come across needs for low-level services that they cannot meet. Do they record these and tell managers or policy makers that these needs remain unmet? Or do they think this is not worth the bother?

We asked social workers and nurses in separate surveys which, if any, of a series of ordinary life activities they might record as an unmet need if an older person being assessed could not undertake it for her/himself (see Table 1).

Not surprisingly, personal care is an example of near unanimous agreement, with 28 of 32 social work respondents stating this would constitute an unmet need if it could not be met. However, at one extreme, one social worker said that only an unmet need, to get in or out of bed, would be recorded.

Table 1 Items recorded as unmet need by social workers if an older person could not undertake the activity for him/herself (n = 32)

Activity	No. of social workers
Shopping	24
Gardening	12
Housework	23
Social trips	19
Housing repair jobs	13
Changing curtains	10
Looking after oneself	28
Going to an adult education class	14
Going to a religious service	17
Going on holiday	12
Getting in/out of bed	27

More widely, there was no consensus over what should be classed as unmet need. A third to a half of social workers thought that social activities and household tasks should be included as unmet needs. Clearly, social workers do not have an exhaustive wish list but are cautious in seeing something as a 'need'.

One respondent wrote:

> The examples I have ticked 'no' to should be regarded as needs – however my local authority regards them as wants rather than needs.

Another confirmed that the departmental view prevailed:

> It is difficult to agree on a definition of 'unmet need' and some of the above would be controversial to my department, e.g. changing curtains/ housework.

In other areas social workers had been told not to record such items as needs, for example, one observed:

> We have been advised when completing unmet needs that we no longer record cleaning/shopping or housework. Social services can no longer provide these services.

We asked nurses whether it was the Government's responsibility to meet any or all of the same activities, adding two further items that were suggested to us by our older people's research group as being of particular relevance to nurses: help with cutting toenails and bathing (see Table 2).

Table 2 Nurses who consider that the State should be responsible for meeting activities that an older person cannot undertake (*n* = 37)

Activity	No. of nurses
Shopping	28
Gardening	8
Housework	30
Social trips	11
Housing repair	22
Changing curtains	7
Looking after oneself	37
Going to an adult education class	5
Going to a religious service	9
Going on holiday	5
Getting into/out of bed	37
Cutting toenails	36
Help getting in/out the bath	37

Nurses thought that some areas were clearly the responsibility of the State if a need existed: getting into and out of bed; bathing; looking after oneself; and cutting toenails. There was less support for assistance with holidays, changing curtains, gardening and going to adult education classes or a religious service. Housework and shopping were also considered by most as something where assistance should be available if needed.

Some respondents noted that they would support state responsibility in areas where there were distinct health-related connections: shopping if it promoted a healthy diet; gardening if it reduced danger; or housing repairs if they promoted safety. One person suggested that support with attendance at an adult education class should be available if it provided medical information.

Only two of the 37 considered that there was sufficient low-level support: one worked in day care, the other in a nursing home. Another noted that many of these types of support were available to those older people who could pay for it.

In the light of the nurses' extensive contact with older people with high levels of illness, disability or health problems we asked their three priorities for low-level support (see Table 3).

Table 3 Priorities identified by nurses ($n = 37$)

Priority	No. of nurses
Personal care	21
Help in/out bed	14
Shopping	11
Help in/out bath	10
Help with housework	10

Other priorities included: day centres, reducing isolation, overnight toilet care, better meals on wheels and more organised voluntary services. No one thought going to an adult education class or having curtains changed was a priority.

They were asked who should be responsible for the provision of low-level services: statutory sectors (NHS, local authority), voluntary, commercial or family sources. They could select multiple options (see Table 4).

Table 4 Responsibility for low-level services ($n = 37$)

Provider	No. of nurses
Families	29
Local authorities	27
Social services	27
Voluntary sector	19
Health (NHS)	16
Commercial sector	10

Nurses were asked whether their own role might include more low-level support. A minority of 12 thought this might be possible. Most of these agreed that the benefits would lie in areas such as:

- early detection of physical, mental and social problems
- enhanced quality of life for people
- promotion of health, less illness and demand
- initiate (hospital) discharge sooner.

In part the reluctance to add low-level tasks to their role stemmed from limited funding. One noted the problem of 'adequate resources and funding' and another mentioned the shortage of nurses.

Nurses were asked what they did if they came across an older person with an unmet need for low-level support services. Would they undertake any of four courses of action (see Table 5)?

Table 5 Nurses' reported actions on learning of unmet need (n = 37)

Action	No. of nurses
Flag it up within own service	19
Refer to local authority	19
Refer to voluntary group	18
Explain that they were unable to help	3

Their responses were influenced by what they saw as shortages in the local authority/social services sector, for example:

> Social services care has been cut to the bone. Clients who require low-level support don't always qualify for help – just helping to alleviate the worry of coping will keep the older person healthy longer and therefore independent and not having to be funded for residential care.

> Social services often offer a very limited service. I feel they could offer more low-level support. We use the voluntary sector and families to fill in the gaps. Lack of support can result in a patient having to move into residential care.

> Many low-level needs go unmet, although not unrecognised. Social services are so restricted in terms of what they can do. There is a need for a low-level support group.

However, other sources of support were also seen to have problems in responding. One nurse noted:

> Volunteers are a 'dying breed' as everyone mostly works and then wants to have time to themselves – myself included!

Another acknowledged:

> Rural transport is a problem. Younger members of family live away, have to work, can't give low-level support.

Finally, a retired nurse, the former carer of both her parents and carer for a disabled friend with whom she had lived for the past eight years, wrote of some of the difficulties experienced in receiving support: staff having to rush off after half an hour even when this was not long enough to provide personal care and breakfast.

In Table 6 we put the responses of social workers and nurses alongside each other, recognising that there were differences in the focus of the surveys and the questions.

Table 6 Comparison of social workers' and nurses' responses

Activity	Social workers Would record as unmet need if person could not undertake for self	Nurses State should be responsible if person could not undertake for self
Shopping	24	28
Gardening	12	8
Housework	23	30
Social trips	19	11
Housing repair jobs	13	22
Changing curtains	10	7
Looking after oneself	28	37
Going to an adult education class	14	5
Going to a religious service	17	9
Going on holiday	12	5
Getting in/out of bed	27	37
Cutting toenails		36
Help getting in/out the bath		37

Both nurses and social workers considered that personal care (getting in and out of bed and looking after self), housework and shopping were key activities. The two items specifically included in the nurses' survey (toenail cutting and help with bathing) were accepted as important by virtually all the nurses. Nurses made clearer distinctions between the services that the State should and should not support. Higher percentages of nurses than social workers thought there should be support for the tasks listed above that both groups saw as core, though nurses also gave more emphasis to housing repair. However, nurses gave much less weight to attending religious services and what might be seen as social activities: social trips, holidays and adult education classes.

Both nurses and social workers revealed difficulties in meeting people's needs and recognised that these could lead to problems in staying at home or leaving hospital care. Nurses thought that families should help with low-level support where possible but that other agencies had responsibility, particularly the local authority.

One respondent in the survey of local authority social work staff had noted that there was a tendency for practitioners 'not to raise expectations or record needs that they know will not be met'. Those leading the seven group discussions with older people, similarly, were mindful of the fact that the very act of holding the discussions might lead people to think that more services were to be made available.

4 Systems and services: current practice

Focus on prevention and preventive services

By the end of the 1990s, the Government announced a specific policy focus on independence as the objective of services. This recognised the importance of preventive services in sustaining independent living to include not only those older people that were at the boundary of residential care or acute hospital care but also those who were at risk of losing their independence more generally, such as by having to stay at home instead of participating in the local community. Special grants were announced – the *Partnership Grant* and the *Prevention Grant* (later becoming the *Promoting Independence Grant*) – to support this shift in policy. These grants gave local authorities the opportunity and a small amount of resources to deliver 'low-intensity' or 'low-level' support services and to stimulate the development of preventive strategies, so targeting 'low-level' support services for people most at risk of losing their independence.

Examples given are of moving into a new home, practical skills such as paying bills and budgeting, befriending and companionship, developing social links, schemes that help people with domestic tasks both inside and outside the home, and general advice and information on services and resources within the community. As will be evident, many of these are provided under *Supporting People*, often through local authorities' housing services, rather than social services provision (ODPM, 2004). This raises questions about co-ordination of assessment and support planning with social services, and about the reality of the separation of 'need' from housing benefit.

For this report we have collected information from older people, social workers and social care managers, and nurses. Given that many people approach social services for help, there is a danger of assuming that most relevant need among older people already passes under the noses of social services – concerning either people accepted for some sort of service or people who are declined a service. This is not necessarily the case, as Patmore (2006) comments.

- People in sheltered housing may bring *some* such needs to *Supporting People*; sheltered housing wardens are obvious potential contact points/brokers for many types of common need among those older people who live in sheltered housing.

- People in council or housing association housing may bring *selected* needs to housing staff.

- Most important of all, there are many older people who do not take common needs to social services or housing providers. They may approach Age Concern, private services, general council enquiries. Any solution must include elements that they can readily access.

Wenger (1992) has reported on the significance of networks in older people's lives in meeting needs. Of course communities vary in the types of personal network most common among their older residents. In some there will have been little movement and long-established family and friendship patterns of support. In others, where older people have moved later in life, or younger people have moved away, there is little available support.

Recognising the importance of this wider context, we nevertheless concentrate in the next section on social services' provision.

Working in social services: the practice of provision

In the following sections we draw on material from our surveys of local authority social services' departments. In summary, the following points arise from the detailed responses that we received.

- The term *unmet need* has been bypassed by some authorities, with *presenting* and *eligible need* coming to the fore (see Box 7 below).

- Practitioners record things differently, some only noting a shortfall when they judge it to be the responsibility of the authority to ensure the service is provided.

- Practitioners are anxious not to raise people's expectations.

- Knowledge of those people who are offered advice at an initial screening stage, rather than being given an assessment, is likely to be lost. The advice may not be recorded; there is unlikely to be a record of what the individual does in response to this advice.

- The authority may want to know what presenting needs are not met, but may find it difficult to gather, rely on, collate and use this information.

- The new single assessment process may help to ensure more thorough and less repeated assessments but there is no essential link between what is found out at assessment and what is provided.
- FACS (*Fair Access to Care*) guidance has established a clearer relationship between what is needed and what an authority can afford.
- However, the guidance is not focused on prevention in general, but on preventing people moving into higher categories of eligibility.

Box 7 When is a need not a need?

- *Service deficit* records that an agency has failed to supply a service that it recognises should be provided; the service may be available to some people but not all, or may not be available to anyone.
- *Service shortfall* may simply note that a service does not exist, without the recognition of obligation; alternatively, it might denote a service that is being delivered but not in the volume required either by client or commissioner.
- A *presenting need* suggests that something is put forward as a need, whether by the older person, a relative or a worker.
- An *eligible need* is clearer: a worker, on behalf of a local authority, has recognised that a person is eligible to have his or her need met.

An overview

We have pieced together the responses from one anonymous local authority to several questions in our survey to present a discussion of many of the key factors that are pertinent to our discussion. It said:

> Some practitioners are proactive in providing advice and information or direct referral to local non-statutory provision to meet needs that are not met by social care services. In order to usefully use information to inform strategic planning or service commissioning the right data sets need to be established, plus consistent inputting. This is an area that requires more attention than at present.
>
> Advice and information is also given by *[our]* Social Care Direct *[screening]* service in response to 'low-level' needs identified at this point. However there is no follow-up, so it is unknown whether individuals get their needs met in this way.

The Community Care team as a whole looks at a range of performance information available. More detailed analysis is undertaken from time to time on specific issues, either on an ongoing basis or as part of specific projects. *[It would be useful to ask]* 'Who is responsible for ensuring that the correct data is being collected?'

We are looking to understand what presenting needs we are not meeting in order to identify how we might help prevent or delay the need for statutory services. This work should help indicate and predict future demand for preventative 'low-level' services. A range of services was established using the Prevention/Promoting Independence Grant including advocacy, day care, home improvement agency/handyperson/ home safety audits, falls prevention schemes *[exercise programmes]*, befriending schemes *[telephone and visiting]* etc. These are usually commissioned from voluntary organisations. Further services have been developed including gardening programmes but these are limited due to resource constraints in both management development time and monitoring. In addition there are a number of preventive services provided through the grants to voluntary organisations.

A prevention strategy has been agreed that focuses on needs that fall below the FACS threshold in terms of service provision by social care, i.e. development of services in communities that are easily accessible and affordable. They intend to support older people to remain at home and promote independence (i.e. choice and control).

The new FACS guidance from the DH *[Department of Health]* makes a much firmer link between 'needs' and what councils can afford. The idea of an absolute, human definition of need has effectively now gone in policy terms and the concept of 'unmet needs' now sits in a very different context, moving from being a professional debate to a political one. This has made it simpler for consumers to understand and the issue of the level of social care funding, more transparent. *[Our]* policy has been to sustain the current level of funding for social care and older people in the face of severe funding constraints on the authority, in part caused by changes in central government funding formulas.

Prevention and FACS: Often people talk about 'preventative' in a broad sense, preventing falls or ill health, etc., whereas, because FACS focuses the resource issues around the individual and their assessed needs, it only really relates to 'preventing' needs falling into higher bands. The

> phasing out of the special ring-fenced prevention grants reinforced this and was a backwards step. FACS actually makes it more difficult for social care to hold onto ring-fenced funds for broadly targeted preventative services, accessible without assessment.
>
> *Recording needs:* We are having to ensure that people who do not look like they are going to be eligible are not screened out early on in the process. Also to make sure practitioners record needs that do not look like they will be eligible. We have stressed we wanted these recorded, not least because it is the only way we could work out what a change to the current threshold would mean and cost. The tendency is still for practitioners not to raise expectations or record needs that they know will not be met.

Drawing on the material from the other respondents to our survey, we discuss these topics in more detail.

Recording and collating information

The detailed responses make clear that there are two main routes into finding out what it is that people need and is not provided, which for the purposes of this part of the report we shall continue to term *unmet need for low-level support*. The first is that information on such unmet need *may* be recorded on the assessment forms of individuals. The second is that various other ways are constructed to try to find out what people want. One authority is trying to ensure that records will be kept about older people whose needs are not 'severe enough' to be categorised as 'eligible' for any service.

Assessment forms

The overriding picture is that there is little valuable information on unmet need that is gained from individual assessments. Although most respondents to our survey recognise the gaps in their own systems, which mean that many people wanting low-level services will not be assessed, whether or not staff are expected to record unmet need for low-level services, this rarely happens. Moreover, the data that exists is rarely aggregated, sometimes because IT systems do not allow this:

> In formal terms, *[collecting data on unmet need]* is very limited at present because this data is not currently captured in departmental assessment, care planning or review processes. This is being addressed in the

> implementation of new care management arrangements (which are also encompassing Single Assessment Process [SAP] implementation).

However, others note that the information is 'recorded on client care plan' and that 'Once an unmet need is identified by assessors the team manager completes an unmet need form'. One authority reported a structured scheme:

> Local Area Teams have Service Solutions teams who collate individual needs/gaps from assessment info. The Service Solution Teams meet with strategic commissioning staff who have analysed Area Team activity to identify strategic gaps, e.g. need for more extra care housing, intermediate care, etc.

The formal systems that have been introduced in some authorities do not always work effectively:

> We have forms called 'lessons for services' which Practitioners can complete as the outcome of an assessment but in reality they rarely do. We tend to rely on more anecdotal descriptions of unmet need made at forums such as team managers' workshops.

Where information is drawn from individual assessments it is apparent that, as in the example above, frequently staff are relied on to remember information and make use of it in meetings:

> Reports from Group Managers to Partnership Boards based on feedback from practitioners.

> Informal only via team meetings, etc.

One authority provided detailed information of the ways developed to link better recording with better commissioning:

> *[Our authority]* has recently established a pilot system of recording assessment outcomes. This will assist in aggregating information relating to service user needs to be used to inform patterns of need across the authority and inform the commissioning of services.

> The system also records an outcome against an intervention to demonstrate whether this has been successful and the service user's needs met to their satisfaction.

The information is recorded as a code, on the service user's care plan through the computerised information system. Each area of the care plan is able to produce information which can be aggregated and analysed either as stand-alone data, or in relation to other factors. Review codes also allow fieldworkers to record why a service has been changed/ cancelled; where dissatisfaction has been expressed or success achieved.

Further work is being taken forward in the pilots to:

- develop a process of feeding in the assessment outcomes to contribute to the Directorate's Performance and Business framework *[and]* … contract management;
- train staff in the use of new codes.

Surveys, consultation and data analysis

Recognising the gaps in the information available to them, most authorities reported they are developing additional ways of gathering information about services that are wanted:

- census data, including a comparison between census data and levels of services that could be predicted, population analysis, deprivation statistics
- service users' complaints
- contract monitoring
- consultation and user surveys, service user groups
- benchmarking
- shortfalls for certain services – waiting lists, delays in hospital discharge
- picking up on people awaiting assessment
- budget analysis
- performance indicators

- allocation panels
- liaison with voluntary agencies, e.g. Age Concern is funded for a well-check service
- Social Services Inspectorate (currently Commission for Social Care Inspection) inspections.

Sometimes these are one-off events, sometimes regular occurrences. The energy that is put into these exercises appears impressive, though we have no way of knowing the effectiveness of such approaches in discovering older people's unmet needs for low-level services. Three comments provide additional information about different systems in three local authorities:

> We have a low-level service called Care Network. The assessors on the front desk of the service collect information about unmet need. Care Network services are accessible, affordable and quality assured and provided by the not-for-profit sector.
>
> The *Supporting People* programme has piloted a Housing and Support Needs Form as a means of capturing this information directly from individuals who approach services such as local authority housing and various service providers.
>
> ... extensive consultation with service users, carers, staff, health agencies, voluntary and independent sector on how to improve services and identifying gaps/unmet need.

Some respondents suggested reasons for not collecting data on unmet need for low-level services. The first of these reasons was their concern that information on unmet needs might be seen as requirements that the authority had failed to meet. The second was that, given that there were insufficient funds to meet current demand, what justification could there be for collecting information on further services that could not be provided?

The detailed information added by many respondents to the requests for 'Yes/No' answers brings out the complexity of the topic. Most people claimed their authorities did aggregate data, and that it was used for strategic planning and service commissioning. The detailed responses show the limitations to the collection and use of data. Over three-quarters of respondents stated that the data they had was not systematically analysed, nor was it taken to multi-agency planning groups at which service users or carers were present. Over half replied that the data was not seen by councillors. Given that it is councillors who make the funding and budget settlements, one might have expected these numbers to be higher. Arguably such data might play a significant part in determining local budget approvals.

Nevertheless, many respondents did think their planning and commissioning strategies were influenced by local information, as one illustrated:

> We have developed a comprehensive integrated commissioning strategy for older people 2003/06 which is reviewed on an annual basis to ensure any local and national changes/influences/needs are incorporated and provides an update on key targets.

Others wrote that information collected locally had been used to:

- map need and planning services
- develop a brokerage service
- influence methods of contracting
- identify areas where there were unmet needs for domiciliary care
- produce a range of integrated health and social care services which could provide an appropriate and timely response
- strengthen our ability to obtain service solutions at a local level.

Several authorities reported attempts to develop strategies that themselves form the basis for further consultation, for example:

> Countywide commissioning strategies are drafted for a three-year period for each major user group. These are used as a basis for consultation with other agencies in the relevant countywide Strategic Partnership and with independent sector providers, in order to clarify respective responsibilities in meeting needs and plan services accordingly.

One authority uses data collected via 'unmet need monitoring' to examine the whole range of services:

> Unmet needs monitoring through staff feedback in particular has helped the service specification for low-level support/social contact scheme as inappropriate requests to home care had been identified as well as

feedback through consultation on the need for preventative services. Unmet needs work has also helped with the business case for developing extra care housing. Unmet needs monitoring has identified shortfalls in provision around supported accommodation and daytime opportunities.

Low-level support services

We asked what low-level support services had been provided under *Fair Access to Care Services*. The list we collected is extensive and illustrates many attempts to plan for needs as they have been perceived for particular groups of people in particular localities.

Box 8 Low-level support services provided under *Fair Access to Care Services*

- Advocacy: Alzheimer's Group.
- Day care: low-level day care run by five voluntary groups across different ethnic groups.
- Hospital advocacy support.
- House management, repair and improvement: home improvement agency; handyperson; home safety audits; care and repair; Anchor 'Staying Put'; Age Concern 'Safely Home' scheme.
- Falls prevention schemes (exercise programmes).
- Befriending schemes (telephone and visiting); telephone companionship service with Age Concern; peer support and befriending with Alzheimer's Society; companionship service for the cared for – to give carers a break; tender under way for social contact scheme.
- Low-level domiciliary care and non-personal care.
- Information service via a disability organisation to signpost and give advice on all aspects of disability issues.
- Equipment centre with advice for people who have low-level needs.
- Sitting service.
- Respite care.

Continued

- Daily driving.
- Hospital Accident and Emergency department (A&E) case finding project with Age Concern.
- Community Furniture Service – a decorating and handyperson service.
- Self-help support for people with mental health needs through MIND.
- Service user and carer empowerment group.
- Holiday and Opportunities Fund for carers.
- Social services department directly provided Community Support Workers for people with dementia and carers.
- Community meals services.
- Home bathing service.
- Laundry Service.
- Shopping and pension collection.
- Communication guide service for deaf/blind people.
- Home from hospital service.
- Funding to enable more people to have access to information technology.
- Luncheon clubs.
- Supporting People funds to develop floating support.
- Fund nurse working in residential care to promote health; fund carers' nurse to access and promote health needs of carers.
- Carers' grant allocated currently to a range of preventative and integrated day services (Age Concern and centres primarily used by black and minority ethnic community).
- Short breaks in the home (frail older people).
- Black and minority ethnic outreach and support service.
- Benefit advice/debt counselling.
- Leisure and education services.
- Live at Home Scheme, The Stroke Association, Parkinson's Disease Society activity group, Age Concern interest circles, bereavement care.

Contined overleaf

- The Carers' Grant supports low-level services for older people and their carers: chat line/telephone ring-out services, primary care information (link worker), health care work and carers' website.
- Good neighbour scheme.
- Housing-related support services for older people and the extension of community alarm services.
- Warden scheme in place; enhanced warden schemes.
- Community-based quality of life activities – e.g. healthy eating; exercise; lifelong learning; community engagement and volunteering; community-based volunteer information and advice.
- Funding to voluntary sector for transport, welfare benefits advice, handyperson, safety in the home, lunch clubs, carers' groups, black and minority ethnic service user lunch clubs, gardening, shopping, visiting services.
- Assistive technology.

It is important to note the increasing emphasis being given to *prevention* as a term that can expose the purpose of a low-level service:

> The provision of prevention type services is seen as an essential part of the strategic commissioning and service development of older people services. They have been incorporated into the whole-system older people's strategy and the integrated commissioning strategy.
>
> We need to be much clearer about understanding what 'prevention' is – it isn't just about providing the same service in smaller portions at an earlier stage. It should be about equipping people with the skills, coping techniques and circumstances to remain independent. It's as much about learning how to use a computer, pursuing an active lifestyle or ensuring a safe neighbourhood, etc., as it is about providing one hour of home care per week. It's a responsibility that extends well beyond social services.

However, the other side of the picture is budgetary constraints:

> The current council culture is one of cuts and meeting essential need. Preventative services are currently a low priority because of the lack of funding. Need to improve on whole-systems approach in the council,

which looks at how leisure, lifelong learning, etc. takes needs of older people into account.

Earlier assessment

We have already noted one local authority's view that improved assessment would not necessarily lead to improved services to address unmet needs for low-level services. However, nearly all the authorities that responded took a different view, contending that they would be better able to:

- provide joined-up, preventative services
- rely on the information that emerged, as it would be more consistent and less subjective – needs should be more explicit
- aggregate data on unmet need with new IT systems
- co-ordinate better the information obtained from different places and agencies
- signpost people earlier to other agencies
- look at the needs from a holistic or whole-system perspective – indeed from the perspective of the person
- lead to better identification of expertise through more integrated ways of working.

Views from the front line

We have further information from our survey of front-line practitioners working directly in social care. This helped to assess the validity of the responses above. Twenty-four of the 31 social work respondents told us that their departments provided a way for practitioners to report the presence of unmet need if this was discovered in an assessment of an older person. A minority worked in areas where such a system was not developed. For example, one stated:

> No official methods of recording unmet need – it is up to individual practitioners to ensure the service users' unmet needs are clearly outlined in the assessment documentation.

Twenty of the social workers said they received feedback on their reports of an unmet need. However the nature and extent of this feedback varied as these examples illustrate:

> Recognition that there is an unmet need.
>
> Yes, we do get feedback via admin staff.
>
> This is only recorded on the case file.
>
> Collated on database but relies on accurate logging of unmet needs.

Others wrote that they received no feedback:

> We get no feedback on what happens to this information once we have collated some and passed on to our managers.
>
> Not directly, but often via gradual development of new services.

A few social workers considered that things might change, for example with a:

> … new pilot and service solutions team and a new commissioning model based on localities and the electronic single assessment forms.

Another wrote that s/he received feedback 'occasionally – a great change from past times when senior managers were not interested'.

Other responses raised the question of whether such unmet needs might feature in the assessment process, or were perhaps not classified as needs before any assessment was conducted. For example, one considered that the important issue was about the role of:

> … adequate admin*[istrative]* support on the front line, supporting those doing assessments of needs – often the information is known but staff have no time to record unmet needs – survival, and what is available in place, takes precedence.

Another commented:

> Some social workers seem to be adopting a lazy 'tick-box' approach to needs assessment, rather than a holistic approach.

Others reported that older people they assessed were sometimes highly likely to see some items of need as extremely important, for example:

> Gardening may only be an issue only part of the year. However most of my clients have seen this as a priority.

Another added:

> Any or all of these *[possible support tasks listed in our questionnaire]* could be identified as unmet need, as self-assessed by the older person or carer. Depends how important each 'need' is to the individual and what the impact would be in having the need met.

Social work respondents were asked about their knowledge of what happened to the information they provided on unmet need within their social services departments. Not everyone was confident that they knew:

> As far as I am aware, little attention is paid to unmet need anywhere in the organisation.

Another was rather more cynical:

> I am told the information is used to plan future services but no report regarding this is issued.

Front-line practitioners have not had great opportunities to influence debate, although some research has established their perceptions about targeting of services on those most in need and the consequences for low-level or preventive services (see, for example, Postle, 2002). The survey reported here was small-scale and asked practitioners for their views rather than observing practice and its outcomes. Nonetheless, these responses indicate areas that may be of particular relevance to current debates and we outline these three areas below.

1. Practitioners are under no illusion that low-level services are readily available. They consider that social services' eligibility criteria are high and that older people's needs are often unmet.

2. While assistance with personal care is not a low-level need, many practitioners find that this is not met adequately. Services such as help with shopping are viewed as important in helping older people remain at home. Few practitioners consider that services are meeting needs for social activities or similar.

3 As we have seen, nurses responding to our survey did not consider that the NHS or commercial sector should take on low-level support. They see this as a responsibility of local authorities (not differentiated from social services), the voluntary sector and families.

Low-level service provision in partnership

A growing number of councils with social services responsibilities (CSSR) and partner agencies are acknowledging the benefits of commissioning low-level support services from, or grant funding to, the voluntary and community sector. Increasingly these are partnership arrangements between adult social care services, primary care trusts (PCTs) and district councils. Similar partnerships can be used by the voluntary and community sector to attract national funding streams, such as European Social Fund monies.

We were told about schemes that varied from handyperson schemes to those that encourage learning IT skills, and from telephone befriending to opportunities for volunteering, such as time banks that encourage reciprocity in communities.

The benefits of drawing on several funding streams were apparent to commissioners and funders in providing 'value for money' services and being able to promote their respective agendas.

- Local authorities: links with Local Public Service Agreements (LPSAs) and the developing Local Area Agreements (LAAs), together with Green Paper (Department of Health, 2005a) outcomes – for example, quality of life and increasing volunteering opportunities.

- Public health: well-being agendas – priorities in the *Choosing Health* White Paper (Department of Health, 2005b).

The community care assessment process should take into account individual resources and capacity to make those changes required as well as social support and exclusion issues. In practice, social workers in community care teams now experience something quite different. Their role is to assess needs and provide a package of care services and so is focused on the 15 per cent of older people who are eligible for services. Almost invariably, care packages are made up of services procured through block contracts and consist of traditional services that support personal care needs such as home care, meals, day care and residential care. 'Spot purchases', that is services that are tailored to meet individual needs, are rarely, if ever, available. The only route to such individualised services seems to be via Direct Payments, which practitioners do not always promote and older people are sometimes fearful to try.

Consequence of FACS

It is current practice that a community care assessment is focused on meeting those personal care needs deemed to be 'critical' or 'substantial' (*Fair Access to Care Services* eligibility criteria), though 'low'-level needs, including practical and emotional support, are often met by a formal care package.

While community care assessors in social services departments tend to be consistent in their interpretation of critical and substantial needs, and the risk to a person's health and safety, the risk to community inclusion and relationships is felt to be more open to interpretation.

Time constraints are likely to prevent social care staff from proactively seeking alternative 'low-level' preventive schemes that might meet an individual's needs in a more tailored way within a care package to meet eligible needs. Similarly, staff say they are encouraged to use block pre-purchased services, including residential care, when the cost of an alternative care package consisting mainly of home care reaches a notional ceiling, though this would seem to contravene guidance.

The same time constraints apply when ineligible needs are identified that cannot be addressed within the care package, in that practitioners neither consistently record nor help find solutions to meet 'low' or 'moderate' needs.

Accessing low-level support services

Reception and screening services for social care services offer the first point of contact for potential service users and carers. People can be 'screened out' of statutory services and 'screened in' to low-intensity preventive services; alternatively they can be advised how they can meet their own needs, for example through the purchasing of equipment to promote independent living.

FACS eligibility criteria state that anyone who appears eligible for community care services is entitled to an assessment of their needs. Referrals that meet these eligibility criteria can be passed on to the most appropriate community care team.

While social workers should have been trained (or retrained) to conduct community care assessments and apply the FACS criteria, staff in screening and reception services may not have been. It is possible that they are still operating to the 'gatekeeping' model with a medical model approach that is functionally orientated: 'Can you wash, dress, get to the toilet?', while they make a judgement about both the nature of the problem and the degree of risk.

Information about alternative services offering low-level support is often reliant on local knowledge and experience. Robust systems are unlikely to be in place to manage or update knowledge, so dissemination can be both fragmented and haphazard.

The dilemma facing practitioners is highlighted. They may appreciate that FACS can be used to argue the case with their managers for meeting low and moderate needs, since guidance states:

> Where funds allow, services to prevent higher-level risks will be provided. This will be in situations where there is good reason to believe that providing services (including services for informal carers) will prevent needs reaching the Critical and Substantial risk levels).

Yet they are unlikely to be successful in getting the services when cutbacks (too often disguised as 'reviews') are constantly being threatened and implemented.

This being the case, the challenge is to ensure that low-level support services are made universally available and accessible though a variety of routes other than social care personnel. Obvious routes are through the very voluntary and community groups that provide them, such as Age Concern; additionally other voluntary or community organisations offer signposting services. However, the most effective route to accessing services is often by word of mouth from friends, family or neighbours (Hay, 2004) and this may help address the problems of finding people you can trust, which were identified in the group discussions.

Comparative information

McTigue (2005) undertook a study for one local authority of prevention strategies in 15 authorities:

> Six authorities provide social care services for individuals assessed as moderate as well as substantial and critical under FACS. Nine authorities have thresholds at a level where individuals are only eligible for support at substantial and critical levels.
> (McTigue, 2005, para. 3.2)

> All 15 authorities record eligibility decisions on assessment documentation.
> (McTigue, 2005, para. 3.3)

> Seven of the 15 authorities do not have any system to identify and process ineligible need, apart from identifying those needs that are or are not eligible as part of carrying out a full community care assessment. Ineligible needs can be defined as the needs of the wider population or individuals with lower level needs that do not present a high enough risk to individuals for them to be eligible for social care services. In authorities where the eligibility criteria include only substantial and critical levels of need moderate level needs would also be defined as ineligible.
> (McTigue, 2005, para. 3.4)

> All the authorities use the census or some form of demographic information to forecast future eligible needs, though this may not always be related closely to the level of services needed in the future. Some authorities have a more detailed breakdown of this information into localities or relating to a particular service user group.
> (McTigue, 2005, para. 3.6)

Performance and targets

In addition to the perceived erosion of role, social workers state that they experience a preoccupation with bureaucracy, form filling and targets (Rogowski, 2004). Practitioners and service users alike fail to comprehend the relevance of this performance management agenda, seeing the aspirations of their assessments unrealised by the decisions made by their budget-conscious managers.

The increased development of the performance assessment framework (PAF), reviews and assessed packages of care (RAP) and government targets means that many practitioners now see that their managers have a mindset that is focused on performance management culture, and that they are preoccupied with inspection and the consequent reports and star ratings.

Performance management may seem to divert resources to whole teams of performance officers and business managers. There is a risk of losing sight of what should be done. Many practitioners say they now find themselves challenged with using complex IT systems that are not user friendly, are slow to respond and do not support the process. They are also mindful of the time being diverted from service user contact.

However, we are also mindful that 'ineligible' needs are not being recorded as consistently as would be helpful to inform our knowledge of what is not being done as well as what is. Better recording would help with predicting future demand and costing the consequence of not meeting ineligible needs. All data collected needs to be reliably and consistently recorded, otherwise there is no point in doing it. As our surveys show, this is not the case.

Performance indicators have an inherent danger of focusing the energies of an organisation on some factors, with the consequence that others get ignored. If records are kept of the number of bath boards issued (an early indicator), there will be no accompanying record of the number of bath boards that have not needed to be issued because of effective rehabilitation and enablement programmes and practices.

There is also the risk that, with the chase being on for quicker response times to assessments and shorter times for their completion, the quality may suffer. Failing to consider low-level support services may well be one casualty.

A Sure Start to Later Life recognises the importance of low-level services in preventive strategies:

> Our vision is for services to join-up better for older people, for there to be low level services which allow people to remain in their homes, and for there to be better access to information about housing choices.
> (ODPM, 2006, p. 70)

Statements in the report stress the determination that different departments will work closely together in supporting older people. The importance of this agenda would be enhanced if a 'prevention' performance indicator, with targets, were to be developed.

However, it would also be helpful if qualitative indicators were developed that were outcomes based to complement the outcomes set out in the Green Paper, *Independence, Well-being and Choice* (Department of Health, 2005a). This move would help to further our understanding of the benefits of such support to individuals and would provide evidence for additional resources for low-level services.

Attitudes

Attitudes and expectations still influence the climate of social care. Many older people have a practical attitude towards help (as opposed to direct care) and will accept what is available when they need it. However, as we will discuss in Chapter 5, they are unlikely to be aware of the range of services available and do not have a perception of their 'welfare rights' for social care. Some who have tried to get help and have found the process difficult give up, rationalising that there are too many older people for services to go round (di Gregario, 1986). Indeed, one of the main attitudes that social care reception and assessment staff have to counter is that of the low expectations of older people themselves, coupled with the difficulties they experience in asking for and accepting social care services.

The *National Service Framework for Older People* (Department of Health, 2001) has as its first objective the rooting out of age discrimination:

> The aim of this standard is to ensure that older people are never unfairly discriminated against in accessing NHS or social care services as a result of their age ... Social care services will not use age in their eligibility criteria or policies, to restrict access to available services.

Yet it seems that, when considering needs during assessments, areas such as employment and being able to go on holiday are rarely addressed. The individual is unlikely to mention them if the focus of the discussion is on personal care, health and safety.

Yet FACS offers a clear mandate for practitioners to think beyond critical and substantial needs to a more preventive and proactive approach. Further, guidance allows budget holders to resource services where they will prevent deterioration in an individual's circumstances or where there is a threat to independent living. Few practitioners or managers seem to pursue this line.

5 Dialogue and resolution

Living fuller lives

Throughout this report we have highlighted what older people in our study, and those in others, state as to what would help them. This final chapter draws together some of the earlier discussions. We wanted to find out whether the views we had collected seemed to reflect other people's experiences and to get further perspectives on the dilemmas identified. To do this we invited a wide range of people to a consultation event: older people, researchers, practitioners and service managers, voluntary group representatives and community activists. We asked them to read a detailed summary of our work and the Older People's Inquiry report from the Joseph Rowntree Foundation to see if this made sense from their perspectives.

We start by reflecting on some key points before looking at what gets in the way of the provision of the best possible services, noting the perspectives of service providers as well as service users. Following that we draw together some pointers to good practice.

Older people talk about their lives, not services. Thus someone may talk about the joys of seeing children and grandchildren, and yet about feeling lonely or not bothering much with meals since the death of a partner. Alongside this, they may have problems with practicalities – the payment of bills, getting the rubbish out in the proper recycling bins or putting drops in their eyes. 'We all want ordinary living', as one person commented in the end-of-project consultation.

In this report we have returned repeatedly to discussions of services, in particular those provided by statutory services. Yet the concept of 'a good life' takes us far beyond service provision. We argue that any discussion of unmet need should be embedded in a wider vision of developing opportunities for older people to lead fuller lives. We recognise also that some people find it harder than others to participate, whether because of their lack of resources or multiple health problems. Yet, for this report, we must return to the specifics of daily living.

Some older people worry months ahead about Christmas cards and presents, or birthdays. Others who would like to go out for a walk have lost confidence in their capacity or in feeling safe outside. The dilemma they face is that they do not know what should be done. Few want a full-time personal assistant – yet they know that they struggle to manage.

Many of the wants that people have – for example, to have someone shop with them or help them to choose clothes – are very intensive in terms of staff time and reflect perhaps the ways in which social bonds of friendship are less easy to maintain.

Too often a focus on specific problems, and on services to resolve them, neglects opportunities to lead fuller lives. At the end-of-project consultation, people gave examples of communities where older people expanded horizons: groups that went to theatres, museums, walks or swimming and aqua-aerobics. Alternatively, the focus of engagement with someone with dementia may be on their need for personal and home care, not on their need for attachment.

Further, a focus on *prevention* may itself circumscribe developments. Thus, working to prevent falls is a huge improvement on focusing on the treatment of those who have fallen. But a 'preventing falls strategy' may not encourage the raising of one's horizons.

Another policy focus that promotes fuller living is that of maintaining healthy living. So debates about the social care services that people want take place in the context of inadequate funding of community health services.

The words used, together with the meaning ascribed to them, play a significant part in the creation of the social climate.

Of course the provision of a service may provide attachment or exploration of new opportunities. A lunch club may provide a meal and an advice service as well as company. The style and the quality of the provision will affect the meeting of needs that are far subtler than simply providing a hot meal.

Older people from black and minority ethnic communities stress that they want access to the same services as everybody else, but that they also want understanding that some services must be responsive to religion and culture. For some groups this may mean financial support to run a day centre that provides support and advice. Others want to be assured that, whether in a residential home, day centre, hospital or their own home, they will be offered a lifestyle close to that of their choosing.

In later life people recognise their worries about the future and their current concerns. Many minimise problems, wanting to maintain an image of coping that is built on not needing help from others.

Significantly also, older people are only too aware of the intermeshing of their lives inside their houses with the worlds outside, factors to which service providers find it hard to respond. Social care services have tended to focus on personal services within the home. Yet changes to the environment – post offices closing, bus services changing, more expensive adult education classes, pavements that seem unsafe because of cyclists or closures of public lavatories – may mean that older people go out less, exercise less, socialise less and feel less good about themselves. Moreover they may be less able to contribute to family or other social networks. There is strong evidence that people's feelings about themselves and the worlds in which they live affect their sense of well-being and quality of life, which in turn affects their health.

Characteristics of service provision that people value

Finding out about services

People want:

- sources of information that are easily accessible and up to date
- someone to talk to about options
- a system that alerts people to the possibility of support services rather than one that relies on people not asserting themselves – a hidden form of rationing
- monitoring of, or occasional visits to, some older people – a mix of oversight and assessment
- easier access to social services departments, especially by phone.

Assessment

The Single Assessment Process is designed to avoid duplication and facilitate sharing of information. But other elements of assessment are important to older people:

- help to review their circumstances and their options
- possibly continuing contact with a worker, rather than a rushed single interview

- account taken of the interests of two people who are living together, and of carers.

Individual-focused work

We are using a different phrase than 'person-centred' solely to ensure that there is freshness to understanding the significance of the term. Older people want those with whom they come into contact to be focused on them, whether at assessment or in service provision. Whatever systems are used to provide the services, the key for the older person is whether anyone is thinking on their behalf. They value workers who take the initiative to make contacts and sort things out. There are repeated statements from older people that they want staff to work with them who are reliable, able to produce high-quality work and also flexible in that they can respond to changed circumstances. Many older people, although not all, want services from a small number of staff.

Perhaps at the heart of what we are trying to express is whether, when they approach health or social care, older people feel that the practitioners want to help. Too often, people have felt that hurdles have been placed in their way, hurdles that they cannot get over.

What gets in the way of best practice?

Resources

We do not want to fall into the trap that we were specifically asked to avoid by coming to the conclusion that inadequate services are the consequence of a shortage of resources. Yet it is essential that we recognise at the outset that limited resources do have an impact on what can be provided. It is unreasonable to criticise public services for failing to respond to the individual needs of older people without accepting that only so much can be done with the available resources. Three comments from the end-of-project seminar capture this dimension:

> In any debate about low-level needs or unmet need for services we should remember that the needs may arise because many older people do not have the resources to live a good life.

Inequalities early in life affect inequalities in old age.

Society must address wider inequalities.

As part of this recognition, it is essential to highlight also that the rates of pay for direct care staff in social care are at the bottom end of the pay scale – at, or close to, minimum wage levels. There are current problems in the recruitment of staff, which there is no reason to think will do other than get worse.

Having stated the fact that the level of resources has a huge impact on the levels and quality of services provided, we want to put the question to one side, not because it is unimportant but so that we can focus on the key issue that we were asked to tackle. Our interpretation of that question, for the topic of this chapter, is: 'Given current levels of resources, what are the best practices?' We have no doubt that structures, systems and worker style all have a substantial bearing on the quality of provision.

Lack of information

Agencies find it hard to make information accessible and to ensure that it is kept up to date. We have pointed out that provision needs to be more than reactive. People have to be alerted to the fact that there may be information that is relevant to them that they had not expected to find. The problems of providing information have been compounded for social services departments in particular because of fears that they would be even less able to meet demands and, indeed, may be held to account for failure to provide a service that should have been made available.

Reception staff are in the forefront of an organisation's contact with people who want support. They do not play the same role as in a commercial organisation where more trade, in the main, can lead to expansion and higher profits. Whether directly or indirectly, many seem to have imbibed a belief in an impossible task for the organisation, which has led them to try to limit the demands placed on staff. Inevitably, many discourage further contacts.

Thinking and working in boxes

Organisations and departments within organisations have their groups of staff, responsibilities and budgets. It is very clear that simply demanding that a service appear seamless from the user's perspective does not result in that happening.

Workers and managers are concerned about time, workload, budgets and performance targets. It may seem very difficult to share budgets, or spend from one's own budget on a service that, arguably, could come from someone else's funds. Of course there are aspects of 'box working' that make for more work: assessments that are repeated by several staff; having to cope with crises; setting up special meetings that cross boundaries; or having to deal with complaints.

It should be understood also that much of what might be contained in phrases like 'whole-systems' or 'joined-up' working is complex and demanding. Trying to ensure that not only local services but also the local environment all play a part in creating a place where older people can lead fuller lives is not easy. It demands confronting the varying interests of different groups. If older people are going to feel safer walking on pavements, then cyclists have to be engaged, who in turn may argue that traffic on the roads makes it unsafe for them. Keeping open public lavatories that are little used is costly and competes with other demands. A benchmarking exercise by one authority found that more than half of the 15 authorities surveyed did not have a prevention strategy (McTigue, 2005). McTigue further states:

> In general, authorities do not have robust systems in place to measure ineligible needs. Where information is recorded on ineligible needs it is often not collated or used to inform future development.
> (McTigue, 2005, p. 1)

The difficulties of providing some support services

In this report we have stressed repeatedly that the tasks that older people find difficult, and the support that they want, do not fit neatly into service compartments. In a strange way, the more that this is understood by those who plan, commission and provide services, the more complex their task becomes. Who is to provide support services such as accompanying someone to take their pet to the vet or helping someone with the writing of Christmas cards? A second question follows: who is to pay?

A further aspect is equally problematic. If questions about responsibility and payment can be sorted, there remain the practicalities of trying to provide certain services. One person needs drops in their eyes – a two-minute task. How is this to be provided and costed, allowing for travel times?

The difficulty of being a good enough consumer

Many of the systems that are in place presume that the choice of an older person, as a consumer, will ensure that only the best providers of services survive. The reality is that being a competent consumer is not easy and demands energy and experience. The management of services by an individual is complex and personalisation through participation (Leadbeater, 2004) is not easy if you feel your cognitive or physical strength is fading.

Speed of response

Many older people have experienced delays in trying to find out about services, in getting (or not getting) an assessment and in the provision of services. Typically, the delays have been greater in services that have been dependent on assessment by an OT. Consequently, some bypass the assessment system, getting a bath aid or stair rail fitted privately, and know little of what might be available in terms of assistive technology. The risk is that what is fitted may not be the most appropriate system for the individual; however, for some, this solution works well.

Older people's response to problems

Many people think that today's older citizens – in particular those who are over 75 – are more accepting of what is offered than future generations of older people will be. Future generations, the argument runs, have been nurtured in a consumer society and will demand high-quality services. This assumption ignores the fact, when faced with problems such as illness or loss, a person may find it difficult to be a competent consumer. There are large numbers of older people who are depressed and many others who have other mental health problems including suffering from dementia. Neither depression nor dementia makes for a person being a demanding consumer. It is important to add to this that losses, such as bereavement or capacity to manage certain daily tasks, are themselves debilitating and make it less likely that people will want or will have the energy to demand services.

Performance targets

Many staff contend that the focus of performance targets leads away from responsive services. The argument runs that, to allow staff to respond to what individual older people want, they have to be creative. The contention is that the pressure to meet performance targets, whether from politicians and managers, and council tax payers (among whom are older people), works against such creativity. We do not want to add to endless lists of performance targets.

Understanding demand

In order effectively to commission low-level services, funders will have to understand and predict demand. Currently, few local authorities collect and use the data on unmet needs to help with a commissioning strategy. In general, authorities do not have robust systems in place to measure 'ineligible needs'. Where information is recorded on ineligible needs, it is often not collated or used to inform future development.

A number of authorities in the benchmarking study referred to above had developed systems and initiatives to support those with ineligible needs, including networks that co-ordinate the development of new services and comprehensive information and advice to older people to support them to make arrangements.

Accessing services

It is a challenge for older people to get through to the right service and manage the complex systems that they may feel are designed to prevent them from gaining a service. Further, many older people who are given information about a service do not follow it through. Sometimes this is because other aspects of their lives become more important, perhaps their health problems. Or it may simply be that they do not make contact because they hope things will get better for them and that their circumstances may change. Some will be reticent because they lack confidence, perhaps having been refused a service by the statutory sector. They perceive themselves to be less deserving than others. Many older people remain uncomfortable with using current telephone systems, particularly if they have a hearing impairment and so need someone to help them make that call. There may be a role here for the proposed 'navigators' outlined in the Green Paper (Department of Health, 2005a).

Accessibility to low-level preventive services depends on whom older people approach for this information and whether they have an existing source of reliable and trusted information, such as housing managers, wardens, neighbours and friends or a care manager, if they are already known to or have had previous contact with social care agencies. A secondary source seems to be agencies such as Age

Concern or the Citizens' Advice Bureau. The response people get from the first contact is important in determining whether they pursue the service or give up.

The case for low-level services

We think there should be no doubts about the value of low-level services to older people. Baldock and Hadlow (2002) show the impact of services on people's lives:

> Sustaining self-confidence and identity when made housebound by old age is not always compatible with being the best judge of what one needs. Our evidence shows that service interventions sometimes raise morale even where the older person may downplay or even deny their effects. At the same time a lack of help and change to daily routines can have a dispiriting effect. The lesson for care managers and service providers is that they should consider intervening early after a rise in dependency in almost any way that increases an older person's contact with others. They should expect resistance from the older person. Initially there may be as much to be gained by the promptness of intervention as from detailed assessments and the matching of services to needs, particularly where these are likely to delay greater contact with others. (Baldock and Hadlow, 2002, p. 3)

Low-level services need to be reliable and affordable, match what people themselves want and be easy to access. If it is accepted that low-level services are vital to many older people's management of their lives, the questions that remain are second-tier.

- What is wanted?
- How are such services to be provided?
- How are they to be paid for?

The views of social services staff

The views of social services and nursing staff from our surveys demonstrate both frustration with the current position and ideas for improving services. Respondents, who were nearly unanimous about the importance of developing preventive services, noted both the opportunities and the limitations in current developments. Positively, many social services staff think that valuable services are being developed in their areas. We list a few of the schemes mentioned:

> New service just being piloted to provide a 'social support group' to help older people with depression to move onto other mainstream activities.
>
> Once a worker submits a service default form, they receive a written acknowledgement. This acts as an audit trail and encouragement to the worker.
>
> Review of needs of ethnic minority elders: *A Question of Fairness (Age Concern Exeter, 2004).*
>
> We have an agreed ... 'Health and Social Care Protocol' *[to delegate]* health and social care tasks across agencies.
>
> Carers' Holiday and Opportunities Fund.
>
> Funding of pharmacist medication review where problems identified during social work assessment.
>
> The provision of funds for pots of money that community groups can bid for to undertake small-scale projects and activities.
>
> We plan to set up a database of good practice.

In the survey of social workers, respondents provided a range of other suggestions for the development of low-level services, which we have grouped together under three headings:

1. addressing the matter in assessment and care planning
2. establishing a system whereby such information is taken into the social services system
3. achieving a response to such needs.

Addressing unmet needs

The social workers' familiarity with current systems gave rise to a range of ideas for improvement. These included:

> Clearly defined areas of the assessment documentation and a written self-assessment exercise for service users.

Such systems could be fine-tuned:

> The system also needs to record when a need has been met but not in the best way, i.e. shopping done for the person or delivered but they are not able to go themselves.

For some, assessment would need a more extensive process:

> I think the current system is good at assessing unmet physical needs as the assessment is able to pick this up. To pick up social and psychological/emotional 'unmet needs' takes additional time and may not be apparent (fully) on the first assessment visit.

From individual to system information

Some respondents stressed that information needed to be passed into the social services department [SSD] system. One person claimed information on unmet need was:

> Currently recorded only on care plan and seemingly ignored. Should be passed on to strategic planners.

Another observed that, for such a process to be developed, social workers needed to have confidence that it was worth the time:

> Success of *[the]* system depends on staff believing that their record makes a difference to policy makers/service developers. A good way is to allow local and flexible solutions which they can see.

Responding to information

Some of the social workers surveyed said that practice itself would need to respond to any new initiatives:

> I think we should be encouraged to think more creatively, e.g. social trips could prevent depression and need for hospital admission.

Others considered that older people too might like to receive some information on what was happening, even if a need could not be met. One suggested 'A system that generates a formal reply to be sent to the client'.

Social workers stated that they would appreciate better systems to record unmet need and two-way channels of communication. They wanted better feedback on data about unmet need that they supply. Many practitioners implicitly recognised that eligibility criteria are now at extremely high levels. If this is so, in some organisations, discussions of low-level services may appear a luxury if needs, such as those for personal care, are not being met adequately.

The match between official guidance and older people's views

There is widespread agreement between older people's statements of what they want and those from government departments. A recent report from the Social Exclusion Unit (2005) lists what respondents said they needed 'if older people are to enjoy a better quality of life'.

- Joined-up services are key.
- Intervening early is important and investment in low-level prevention can reduce costlier interventions later.
- Older people generally know what they need and want, and they should be involved in the design – and where practicable the delivery – of services.

The authors stress that such factors are important for all older people but of particular importance for those older people who are most at risk of being excluded.

Developing services people want

The key factors

From our own studies and those of others we conclude that there are key factors in the development of better services (our shorthand for the services that better match the wishes and needs of older people):

- involving older people
- involving the whole community
- working with workers
- flexible, individual-focused services – expanding choice of what is available; being responsive.

Involving older people

It is widely acknowledged that services for older people must be designed to suit the user rather than the provider (Law and Janzon, 2004). Systems must encourage participation in the whole process of service development and delivery. Thus, not only may older people need better information, some may also want to produce the leaflets or vet the information that is produced.

At an individual level, there must be greater understanding of how people live their lives and of what they want. It may well take time to help people think through their current circumstances and options. Simply focusing on problems, or even the solutions perceived by an older person, may result in what is provided being limited by current knowledge and expectations. This stage of finding out demands active discussion and negotiation. Most discussion focuses on the wider involvement of older people in planning, developing and monitoring services.

The Older People's Steering Group (2004) from the JRF has set out many of the wider parameters in its powerful report *Older People Shaping Policy and Practice* (2004). Strategies must start with an understanding of older people's lives – services, however important, are only a part of the picture. They demand that older people are seen as citizens, playing important roles in the lives of their families and communities, before stating, drawing on work by Carter and Beresford, that 'Involvement is important at an individual level, as well as being political and collective' (Older People's Steering Group, 2004, p. 56). The report sets out also characteristics of 'meaningful involvement', which requires standards on:

- the numbers of older people involved
- the stage of development when they are included
- their ability to influence the outcomes
- the resources to support them in becoming involved
- their involvement throughout the whole process (Older People's Steering Group, 2004, p. 15).

The authors contend, as would many others, that the experiences and contributions of older people are not central to the process of service development and delivery (Older People's Steering Group, 2004, p. 39). The work of Butt and O'Neil (2004) is quoted:

> Older people from different minority communities said that they were fed up with the message that being Asian, Afro-Caribbean or black was to be 'a problem to be solved'. In fact, many of the day centres in different communities were very alive and active – much more so than some of the more boring day centres provided by the council.
> (Butt and O'Neil, 2004, quoted in Older People's Steering Group, 2004, p. 32)

Others question whether user participation has done much more than influence process (SCIE, 2005, Chapter 9, p. 7).

Involving the whole community

The second theme that we have identified is that of involving the whole community. Huber and Skidmore (2003) have written about *social capital* in contemporary policy-making debates. They quote from the Performance and Innovation Unit's definition:

> ... features of social organisation, such as civic participation, norms of reciprocity and trust in others that facilitate cooperation for mutual benefit.
> (Huber and Skidmore, 2003, p. 66)

Investment in social capital, they argue, is particularly important for older people as some face particular risk of social isolation.

Another central aspect in this theme is that of asserting the place of older people as full citizens, with the rights and responsibilities of all other citizens.

Similarly, the Association of Directors of Social Services and the Local Government Association (2003) have argued for 'inverting the triangle of care', a community strategy to be moved from the bottom to the top of the agenda, referring to:

> Community members, including older people, and agencies working together, taking collective responsibility for promoting the wellbeing of older people and setting priorities.
> (Association of Directors of Social Services and the Local Government Association, 2003, p. 9)

Godfrey and colleagues (2004) relate the experiences of older people to service provision and local communities. They describe the work of a local organisation called Caring Together:

> Rooting itself in the local community and building alliances with existing groups and community activists, it has been able to mobilise the resources of older people in the locality, drawing upon and energising neighbourly networks and reservoirs of reciprocal support towards sustaining people's quality of life, even in the face of restrictions.
> (Godfrey *et al.,* 2004, p. 197)
>
> Caring Together offers opportunities for sociability and friendship, education, social and stimulating activities, mutual support, practical assistance, advice and advocacy across the spectrum of old age.
> (Godfrey *et al.,* 2004, p. 225)

In their views, the value of the group was based on:

- a sense of belonging and being able to help others
- opportunities to engage in social activities and develop new interests and skills
- accessible support and back-up in times of need

- practical help, guidance and advocacy.
  (Godfrey *et al.,* 2004, p. 190)

> The value of all aspects was enhanced by relationships with staff and by the organisation's roots in the local community.
> (Godfrey *et al.,* 2004 p. 198)

Godfrey (2006) has pointed out dilemmas that have developed in the use of voluntary and locality-based groups in meeting 'low-level' needs in one city:

> An interesting development has been the attempt to hive off shopping and cleaning services from the social services department to a social enterprise organisation. There has been considerable pressure on the locality based neighbourhood network schemes to take on this service. This has been resisted by many of them as an attempt to colonise them as 'service' providers, thereby undermining their role as a hub of reciprocal, neighbouring type networks whose prime focus is well-being. The other point about this development – which has been highlighted by the neighbourhood networks – is that it ignores the fact that localities differ in terms of their socio-economic composition and therefore the ability of people to pay for services – impacting on the viability of a provider organisation.

There is a lot of explicit support for such developments. The current round of Local Area Agreements demonstrate this; two of the key related building blocks are Safer and Stronger Communities and Healthier Communities and Older People. Low-level services may then be developed and delivered by and in local communities that understand the need for localism to meet their identified priorities. At a different level, such approaches raise again the question of whether local authorities should rethink their role in the development of communities, a type of collective response that would have been familiar to community social workers, rather than a focus solely on individual need.

Working with workers

Some policy analysts seem to approach the topic of flexible, low-level services by setting out what older people want and then seeing practitioners as the problem, blocking the realisation of older people's hopes. We think this is unhelpful – a core part of any successful strategy will be an alliance between older people, local communities and practitioners. Our own surveys have shown that many workers are frustrated by the fact that they are not able to deliver what they themselves, and older people, would want. One of the attributes rated most highly by older people is that workers treat them as individuals; some like to see staff as more than social workers or care workers. Godfrey and colleagues (2004, pp. 181–2) illustrate this by showing the appreciation that older people had for the practitioners who provided help and the importance of their relationships with them. In addition, they note that in a small community some of the older people had themselves been care workers, and that many of the care workers were known socially to older people and their families.

Hadley and Clough (1996, p. 164) set out a framework of conditions for effective professional work in community care including that 'Relationships with the user are: needs-led; open and honest'. Other important factors cited were: discretion and autonomy; multiple accountability; continuity and security; participation and freedom to speak out.

One of the key factors in the development of person-centred services is that of freeing the potential and creativity of staff to respond flexibly to the older people whom they meet. Sometimes they are not able to do this because budgets are controlled from headquarters, though central government itself both demands increased local control, while directing the ways in which funds are to be spent.

Flexible, individual-focused services: expanding choice of what is available; being responsive

From our own studies, and those of others, we suggest that the following factors are integral to the development of an individual-focused approach.

- Listening to individual older people in a way that searches with them to identify what people want in their lives and which options best match those wants.

- Working with individuals, groups and organisations in local communities to enhance the involvement of as wide a sector of the community as possible in understanding what older people want and the sorts of services that will match those wants. (This takes the first building block and expands it to a local community.)

- Working in ways that maximise the involvement of older people in their communities and these discussions.

- Working with practitioners to ensure their involvement in finding the best possible solutions.

- Trying to ensure that performance objectives and targets drive towards individual-focused services, rather than against them.

Patmore and McNulty (2005) examine factors that promote flexible, person-centred services. They capture ways in which organisational structures constrain responses. Frequently, older people who have home care services talk with the care worker about tasks they would like undertaken or changes they would want to see in the work that is done. Often, the people to whom they talk will be distant from any ability to change what happens. They will be employed by an organisation, which, in turn, has been contracted by a social services department to carry out certain tasks. They set out guidelines for person-centred home care.

- Belief in 'caring for the whole person'; belief in the value of flexible, person-centred home care.

- Customers are served by regular provider staff.

- The provider can deploy some staff time flexibly for *ad hoc* purposes.

- Clear, agreed policies concerning flexibility, use of spare time and assisting customers to find private extra help.

- Purchasers directly commission interventions to address customers' quality of life.

- A pragmatic approach by provider management to decisions on flexible, person-centred help.

- Staff rewards, which can attract and retain high-quality care workers.

- Provider management must be sufficient to ensure basic standards.

- Having enough time is always important (Patmore and McNulty, 2005, pp. 21–4).

They contend that the fundamental factor is the first, requiring that purchasers must believe in the approach and look for providers with like-minded values.

Patmore (2006) has suggested the following might be the components that should be present in any community:

- shopping services
- social centres to create informal information networks
- local authority policies on transport, pedestrianisation, public toilets, adult education, which take older people into account
- services for recommending/introducing plumbers, gardeners, repair services
- commitment for home care services to ensure that very disabled older people can get their mundane practical needs addressed
- a set of informed referral points including social services, housing providers, Age Concern.

McTigue (2005) notes that some authorities have a system to refer to other agencies those people for whom they do not provide a service. One authority had established Care Network, which assists people to get the support they need. Other schemes included a project being developed 'working with the Islamic community to build a self-sustaining community-based service and support network' and 'links with other departments include access to culture and arts giving older people opportunities to go out from day services to access mainstream activities'.

Good-practice clues or strategies

From the information we have collected we have reflected on actions that can take place at different levels in an organisation (see Box 9 below). Solutions do not lie solely in bottom-up or top-down approaches. The drive to understand what someone wants and produce the best support service can come from individual workers or from a Director of Adult Services. To be of any use to the older person, the vision from the top has to be implemented in action.

The authors of the recent review for the Social Care Institute for Excellence (SCIE, 2005) identify the factors that the inspectors (Social Services Inspectorate [SSI] and Audit Commission) have found likely to promote partnerships. They will probably be more successful where they are 'seen as a means to an end rather than an end in themselves'. They work best where:

- there is clarity of shared purpose in user outcome terms
- there is clarity of governance and decision making
- there are wins for each partner
- there are efforts to establish a common culture
- there is explicit agreement about risk and resource sharing
- attention is given to staff development
- there is agreement about the yardsticks for success.

They are less likely to be successful where:

- they are driven purely by national directive
- they are essentially budget driven
- there are major differences of culture and governance (Audit Commission, 2004, pp. 35–36).

Box 9 Three levels of change and elements of each level

Strategic level

- Joint commissioning strategies exist with partners including service users and carers.
- Local priorities have been identified.
- Mapping of the territory, identifying needs that are met and needs that are unmet.
- A culture of prevention is in place, rather than 'fire fighting'.
- A wider policy of helping individuals and communities to live well crosses departmental and organisational boundaries.
- The shifting of the balance of resource allocation enables more funds to be directed to low-level or universal services.
- The 'consumer case' is thought to be as valid as the 'cost-effective' case.

Continued overleaf

- Quality of life factors are given equal weighting to health and safety and personal care.
- Social work skills are recognised as well as care management skills.

System level

- Service users and carers are involved in the design of services.
- Joint funding arrangements or pooled budgets are used effectively.
- There is joint procurement or commissioning.
- A single *service-level agreement* applies to all stakeholders and there is one set of monitoring and evaluation requirements.
- Dedicated staff help to drive this agenda.
- Systems record and collate unmet, eligible *and* ineligible needs.
- Assessors under the Single Assessment Process (SAP), purchasers, provider managers and staff all hold similar values based on an understanding of the whole person.
- Low-level services to people in receipt of Direct Payments and, in the future, those who opt for Individual Budgets are available.
- Self-assessment and self-reviews are developed.
- A culture shift is detectable from, on the one hand, service and resource rationing to, on the other, service and resource choice.
- A database of good practice is created.
- Follow-up letters or telephone contacts are made to people, *whether or not they received services*, so that the organisation stays in touch and checks whether people find solutions to their problems.

Practice level

- There are initiatives to help older people access services.
- Information is easily accessible in various formats – booklets, directories, websites – and in different languages.
- Practitioners acknowledge the importance of low-level services and use them to complement or substitute for statutory services in care packages.

Continued

- Practitioners use the discretion of FACS to meet assessed low- and moderate-level needs.
- Speedy delivery of low-level services for maximum, preventive effect.
- There are small pots of money that can be used for local projects.
- Assessments focus on social as well as physical unmet needs.

Developing individual-focused services

There are examples of the creation of good-practice databases. The London Modernisation Board (2003a, 2003b, 2003c) has a section of its website devoted to the listing of good practice. The Social Policy Research Unit at York has tried to influence practice in community care. A research programme to understand better what users want and what gets in the way of their hopes being realised has been linked to a programme to promote new ways of working. A network of practitioners involved in community care has been established, teaching packs have been developed and tested, and the whole programme has been designed to promote better practice.

Dialogue and resolution

Language and terminology

The terms 'low-level' and 'that little bit of help' have been important in promoting the ordinary and practical services that people want. *Our first conclusion is that they must now be scrapped* because they suggest some services are less important than others. We all have different sorts of needs that intermesh, whether for attachment, practical help or survival. Of course some may be more crucial to health or life itself than others. Yet, the lack of some practical help may impinge far more intrusively on daily living. The term 'low-level' is also ambiguous – 'referring both to particular kinds of services *and* as directed at particular kinds of people' (Godfrey, 2006). She adds that, if one's starting point is well-being, most definitions of low-level services are too narrow: she writes of 'the distinction between the "big problems" that older people experience and the "daily hassles" that they are confronted with on account of disability, loss of energy, flexibility and so on':

> Yet, it is not simply that social care provision is responsive to the needs arising out of the 'big problems' – bereavement, extreme frailty, sudden onset of disability etc., – but only to specific needs – particularly personal care support. But, equally problematic issues arising out of the 'big problems' are risks relating to social isolation, depression, reduction in functional ability that have the potential to make people vulnerable to acute hospital admission or long term care. In what respect then are they 'low level' needs?
>
> But seeing service solutions to social isolation as being simply about day care – since that is what social services offer – is too limited. At the same time, the 'daily hassles' could reflect the ongoing day-to-day difficulties of life flowing out of the 'big problems'. Thus, sorting out the leaky tap may be a difficulty for a bereaved woman whose partner always did those kinds of things. Solutions then might be framed in a range of ways: being given the opportunity to learn new skills; having access to trustworthy tradespeople; or a local handyman service. There is a difficulty about thinking of 'social care services' as being the solution to 'unmet need'. Whilst I think that the report is right in making the distinction between 'eligible' and 'ineligible' need, the challenge is to open out the debate on eligibility but in a way that does not reduce the problem to one of social services' responsibilities or provision through the existing – very limited – service repertoire.

She points out that people will vary in the resources available to them to respond to need (individual, social network and locality) and asks whether and how such factors should be taken into account.

We favour the clarity in terminology of 'eligible' and 'ineligible' services – and the expansion of what is deemed eligible. This should start a debate of what should be eligible, perhaps suggesting the equivalent of the National Institute for Health and Clinical Excellence determining whether a drug should be used in the NHS.

Second, alongside terms such as treatment and prevention, we want to give primacy to well-being. In later life, as at other life stages, citizens should be supported in leading full lives.

Third, rather than talking of older people's needs, we should focus on their rights as citizens.

Entitlement

Ways need to be found to establish agreement and understanding of what citizens should expect in later life. Our conclusions are as follows.

- The real demand for services is depressed because: (a) many people, outside the social care system, do not know about the possibility of services; (b) people choose not to ask for support (to maintain their image of sufficiency; because of past rejections for services for oneself or others); (c) they are made to feel that others are in greater need.
- The real demand for practical support is depressed because so little is available.
- There is disparity in what services are available from one area to another.
- There is too little recognition of the impact of wider changes at central or national levels on the ways in which people live their lives – putting up fees for adult education affects take-up of services.

'The citizenship model stops welfare being seen as something for the very poor', said one participant at the end-of-project consultation. Citizenship is about exercising the rights and duties of being a citizen in society and agreements about what this means should be better developed. Should we, for example, establish minimum levels of service, so that anyone living in any area should be able to call on advice or assistance within a specified time? Should we have entitlements more explicitly set out as, for example, with pensions and benefits? Will the new ideas about individual budgets, which bring together a number of different funding streams from several parts of the public sector, develop a more transparent and clearer system of resource allocation? What happens when people start to talk about the right to get out of the house in old age, instead of what type or quantity of services they need to be delivered to them in their home? Will older people support and pay for the shifts in funding that such changes will require? This point was made by some of the older people we talked to who mentioned the effects of taxation at local levels and of charging on their quality of life.

Citizenship involves responsibility and reciprocity – and this is, of course, true for those in later life.

Working with the wider workforce

Practitioners at the front line, or in middle management, may be overwhelmed by the constraints placed on them as well as by their own awareness of service inadequacies. Yet there are agencies where local or neighbourhood solutions involve workers in being part of the creative forces that bring about improvements. Patmore (2006) contends that a key factor in whether imaginative services develop is the role of senior social services purchasers or commissioners and managers. Do they systematically encourage or discourage? Our staff survey shows the enthusiasm of staff to match better what older people want and that this exists in both social services and health. Integration between the two may be able to build on these shared values.

Finding out about services and support

There are different ways in which people can find out what is available and to what they are entitled, and be helped to think through their own situation. There is a place for good, individualised assessment as a part of a total strategy of finding out and being helped to think about what is wanted. Nevertheless, as we were told in the consultation, 'There is no such thing as a perfect, comprehensive assessment'. Assessment is not the solution to everything that is inadequate in social care or any other services. Our evidence is that it is difficult to find someone to tell you about all the options, and even more difficult to find anyone in a position to help you think through what to do.

Several authorities in McTigue's report (2005) had developed corporate contact centres, sometimes referred to as one-stop shops. These could be valuable in providing information as to available services. However, it is far harder to envisage which people will be able from the perspectives of role, available time and expertise to help people think through their options. The commissioner–provider split has led to an understandable reluctance for social services staff to steer people in a market-driven economy; as we have pointed out the increasing involvement of voluntary sector groups in provision of services means that the impartiality of their role is called into question. Organisations like Age Concern, through partner agencies, provide services such as insurance as well as local services such as day centres and home care. Within statutory services, it is doubtful whether the development of people called 'navigators' will solve all these problems.

The bounds of service provision and responsibility

The support that people may want not only crosses the boundaries of organisations and departments (leisure, education, community safety, social services, health and so on) but also goes outside their traditional boundaries – who is to help someone write a letter or manage their bank account? There are related questions as to the bounds of responsibility for managing different aspects of living. Some people will want support to manage activities for which, previously, they have taken private responsibility. What is the role of the State – in helping people to review their situations, enlarging their horizons, planning services, providing services, monitoring ...?

In the end-of-project consultation, the discussion moved beyond considering how older people got hold of information to the context of 'joining up' information. When people needed a new cooker, for example, if they could not install it or did not have family or friends to help, then they might want to track down a reliable source of help for this. In current service systems, they might have to go to several places to find out who might be able to help, and very few professionals would see this as any part of their advice role. Will new models of support be able to respond to these important needs? As a basis for establishing principles, or as a framework for support, the rights of people as citizens seem sound. Yet there remain complex questions of detail and implementation, such as this one about access.

These are huge questions to which there are no absolute answers. The best hope of answering them comes through the development of local solutions.

Measurement and outcomes

Narrow ideas about what is nowadays termed an 'outcome' may get in the way of simple and understandable improvements to the quality of life. Consultees warned that it was important when looking at the outcome of services or support for this to be undertaken over sufficient time. It was suggested that 'The debate about outcomes has been hijacked into outcomes for commissioning agencies'. By contrast, what matters is people's well-being.

Driving change

We have become convinced that there is no single mechanism or system that will bring about desired changes. Thus creating more choice of services or providers may help some, but not others who do not want to manage as informed consumers. Some groups will present their case better than others.

We have moved from reviewing 'Unmet need for low-level services' to asserting the importance of capturing the complexity of older people's experiences. The services developed should be helping people to lead fuller lives. To do that they must create local collaborations of older people, workers, politicians and service providers from all sectors.

Bibliography

Age Concern Exeter (2004) *A Question of Fairness: An Enquiry into the Health and Social Care Needs of Muslim Elders in Exeter*. Exeter: Age Concern Exeter

Association of Directors of Social Services and the Local Government Association (2003) *All Our Tomorrows: Inverting the Triangle of Care*. London: ADSS and LGA

Audit Commission (2004) *Older People – A Changing Approach, Independence and Well-being*. London: Audit Commission

Baldock, J. (2003) 'On being a welfare consumer in a consumer society', *Social Policy and Society*, Vol. 2, No. 1, pp. 65–71

Baldock, J. and Hadlow, J. (2002) *Housebound Older People: The Links between Identity, Self-esteem and the Use of Care Services*. Research Findings 4. Sheffield: GO Programme

Barnes, M., Matka, E. and Sullivan, H. (2003) 'Evidence, understanding and complexity', *Evaluation*, Vol. 9, No. 3, pp. 265–84

Bradshaw, J. (1972) 'A taxonomy of social need', in G. McLachlan (ed.) *Problems and Progress in Medical Care*. Oxford: Oxford University Press

Clarke, H., Dyer, S. and Horwood, J. (1998) *That Bit of Help*. York: The Policy Press and Joseph Rowntree Foundation

Clough, R. and Manthorpe, J. (2004) 'Unmet need for low-level support: developing a consensus', background report to Joseph Rowntree Foundation, unpublished

Cordingley, L., Hughes, J. and Challis, D. (2001) *Unmet Need and Older People: Towards a Synthesis of User and Provider Views*. York: Joseph Rowntree Foundation

Department of Health (2001) *National Service Framework for Older People*. London: Department of Health

Department of Health (2002) *Fair Access to Care Services – Guidance on Elegibility Criteria for Adult Social Care*. London: Department of Health

Department of Health (2005a) *Independence, Well-being and Choice*. London: HMSO

Department of Health (2005b) *Choosing Health: Making Healthy Choices Easier*, London: HMSO

Department of Health (2005c) *National Service Framework for Long Term Conditions*. London: Department of Health

Department of Health (2006) *Our Health, Our Care, Our Say. A New Direction for Community Services*. London: HMSO

DWP (Department of Work and Pensions) (2005) *Opportunity Age – Meeting the Challenges of Ageing in the 21st Century*. www.dwp.gov.uk/opportunity_age/first_report.asp

di Gregario, S. (1986) 'Understanding the "management" of everyday living', in C. Phillipson, M. Bernard and P. Strang (eds) *Dependency and Interdependency in Old Age – Theoretical Perspectives and Policy Alternatives*. London/Wolfeboro, NH: Croom Helm in association with the British Society of Gerontology

Elkan, R., Kendrick, D., Dewey, M., Hewitt, M., Robinson, J., Blair, M., Williams, D., Brummell, K. and Egger, M. (2001) 'Effectiveness of home-based support for older people', *British Medical Journal*, Vol. 323, pp. 719–24

Godfrey, M. (2001) 'Prevention: developing a framework for conceptualizing and evaluating outcomes of preventive services for older people', *Health and Social Care in the Community*, Vol. 9, No. 2, p. 89

Godfrey, M. (2006) Commissioned paper for Joseph Rowntree Foundation study, unpublished

Godfrey, M. and Callaghan, G. (2000) *Exploring Unmet Need: The Challenge of a User-centred Response*. York: Joseph Rowntree Foundation

Godfrey, M., Townsend, J. and Denby, T. (2004) *Building a Good Life for Older People in Local Communities: The Experience of Ageing in Time and Place*. York: Joseph Rowntree Foundation

Hadley, R. and Clough, R. (1996) *Care in Chaos: Frustration and Challenge in Community Care*. London: Cassell

Hay, J. (2004) 'The accessibility of "low" level preventative services (social care) to older people in Essex to promote independent living', MA dissertation, Anglia Polytechnic University, Chelmsford

Huber, J. and Skidmore, P. (2003) *The New Old: Why Baby Boomers won't be Pensioned off*. London: Demos

Ing, P. with Gifford, S., Grainger, J. and Leese, S. (undated) *Unmet Need: An Audit of the Needs of Community Care Clients*. Stafford: Staffordshire University

JRF (Joseph Rowntree Foundation) (2005) 'Independent Living Committee', www.jrf.org.uk/funding/research/prioritiesandcalls/priorities/independentliving.asp

Law, S. and Janzon, K. (2004) 'Engaging older people in reviewing the influence of service users on the quality and delivery of social care services', *Research Policy and Planning*, Vol. 22, No. 2, pp. 59–63

Leadbeater, C. (2004) *Personalisation through Participation: A New Script for Public Services*. London: Demos

Lewis, H., Fletcher, P., Hardy, B., Milne, A. and Waddington, E. (1999) *Promoting Well-being: Developing a Preventive Approach with Older People*. Leeds: Nuffield Institute for Health

Levenson, R., Jeyasingham, M. and Joule, N. (2005) *Looking Forward to Care in Old Age: Expectations of the Next Generation*. London: King's Fund

London Modernisation Board (2003a) *London Older People's Service Development Programme: Preventive Approaches that Work*. www.london.nhs.uk/olderpeople/paper05.htm

London Modernisation Board (2003b) *London Older People's Service Development Programme: Why Improving Services for Older People and Whole System Approaches are Essential to Meet Key Targets*. www.london.nhs.uk/olderpeople/paper01.htm

London Modernisation Board (2003c) *London Older People's Service Development Programme: Lessons from the Programme – Practical Ideas to Try*. www.london.nhs.uk/olderpeople/paper03.htm

MacDonald, C. (1999) *Support at Home: Views of Older People about their Needs and Access to Services*. Social Work Research Findings No. 35. Edinburgh: Scottish Executive

MacDonald, C. (2004) *Older People and Community Care in Scotland: A Review of Recent Research*. Research Findings No. 35. Edinburgh: Scottish Executive

McTigue, S. (2005) 'Prevention strategy: a benchmarking exercise', unpublished report for Lancashire County Council Adult and Community Services

Manthorpe, J., Cornes, M., Watson, R. and Andrews, J. (2005) *Someone to Expect Every Day, the Partnership Projects in Intermediate Care*. London: Help the Aged

Netten, A., Ryan, M., Smith, P., Skatun, D., Healey, A., Knapp, M. and Wykes, T. (2002) *The Development of a Measure of Social Care Outcome for Older People*. Canterbury: Personal Social Services Research Unit

Nicholas, E., Qureshi, H. and Bamford, C. (2003) *Outcomes into Practice – A Resource Pack for Managers and Trainers*. York: SPRU

ODPM (Office of the Deputy Prime Minister) (2004) *What is Supporting People?* Leeds: ODPM

ODPM (2006) *A Sure Start to Later Life: Ending Inequalities for Older People*. London: ODPM

Older People's Steering Group (2004) *Older People Shaping Policy and Practice*. York: Joseph Rowntree Foundation

Patmore, C. (2001) 'Improving home care quality: an individual-centred approach', *Quality in Ageing*, Vol. 2, No. 3, pp. 15–24

Patmore, C. (2006) Commissioned paper for Joseph Rowntree Foundation study, unpublished

Patmore, C. and McNulty, A. (2005) *Making Home Care for Older People more Flexible and Person-centred*. York: SPRU

Postle, K. (2002) 'Working "between the idea and the reality": ambiguities and tensions in care managers' work', *British Journal of Social Work*, Vol. 32, pp. 335–51

Quilgars, D. (2000) *Low Intensity Support Services: A Systematic Literature Review.* York: JRF Findings

Qureshi, H. and Rowlands, O. (2004) 'User satisfaction surveys and cognitive question testing in the public sector: the case of personal social services in England', *International Journal of Social Research Methodology*, Vol. 7, No. 4, pp. 273–87

Raynes, N., Clark, H. and Beecham, J. (eds) (2006) *The Report of the Older People's Inquiry into 'That Bit of Help'.* York: Joseph Rowntree Foundation

Robinson J. (2004) *Care Service Inquiry Interim Report: Concerns about Care for Older Londoners.* London: King's Fund

Rogowski, S. (2004) 'Are social workers becoming extinct?', *Community Care*, 8 July

SCIE (Social Care Institute for Excellence) (2005) *Developing Social Care: The Current Position.* London: SCIE

Social Exclusion Unit (2005) *Excluded Older People.* London: ODPM

Stewart, K., Challis, D., Carpenter, I. and Dickinson, E. (1999) 'Assessment approaches for older people receiving social care: content and coverage', *International Journal of Geriatric Psychiatry*, Vol. 14, No. 2, pp. 147–56

Sutherland, S. (1999) *With Respect to Old Age, Report of the Royal Commission on Long Term Care for the Elderly.* London: HMSO

Tanner, D. (1998) 'Empowerment and care management: swimming against the tide', *Health and Social Care in the Community*, Vol. 6, No. 6, pp. 447–57

Tanner, D. (2001) 'Partnership in prevention; messages from older people', in V. White and J. Harris (eds) *Developing Good Practice in Community Care: Partnership and Participation.* London: Jessica Kingsley

Tanner, D. (2003) 'Older people and access to care', *British Journal of Social Work*, Vol. 33, No. 4, pp. 449–515

Wistow, G. and Lewis, H. (1997) *Preventative Services for Older People: Current Approaches and Future Opportunities.* Oxford: Anchor Trust

Wistow, G., Waddington, E. and Godfrey, M. (2003) *Living Well in Later Life: From Prevention to Promotion*. Leeds: Nuffield Institute for Health

Walters, K., Iliffe, S. and Orrell, M. (2001) 'An exploration of help-seeking behaviour in older people with unmet needs', *Family Practice*, Vol. 18, No. 3, pp. 277–82

Wenger, C. (1992) *Help in Old Age – Facing up to Change: A Longitudinal Network Study*. Liverpool: Liverpool University Press

Appendix 1: Vignettes

Methods

In order to stimulate discussion with the groups of older people we interviewed, we designed the following composite examples of people who might benefit from low-level support. We found these a good way to get discussion focused on what might happen but also on what should happen. We summarise the main points after each discussion.

Vignette 1

Mrs Doreen Evans lives on her own in a three-bedroom house in a small market town. She recently celebrated her 80th birthday. Generally very well, she has recently started to find some housework chores difficult and the garden is proving hard work. She has recently been diagnosed with early dementia and this news, while upsetting, is something she is coming to terms with. At the moment her memory is not too bad and she uses reminder notes and lists to help. She thinks she might like a 'small bit of help' round the house and garden, but knows that many people are much more in need than she is.

Questions

- What would be your views about who should help Mrs Evans?
- Where should she get this small bit of help?
- Who should pay?

Vignette 2

Mr Gardner is in his early 70s. He is divorced and has lost contact with his family. A heart problem means that he is finding it difficult to look after himself and things are getting a bit neglected round the house. At times he gets depressed and can't be bothered to eat properly or to get dressed. He doesn't want fuss, but does realise that his landlord is not happy with the state of the flat. Some local youths are now hanging round his flat and making Mr Gardner feel a bit uncomfortable.

Questions

- What might be helpful here?
- Should services wait for something to happen or what?
- How can Mr Gardner find help that might be acceptable and from where?

Vignette 3

Mrs Charles is a former nurse who has been looking after her husband since he suffered a serious stroke ten years ago. She has a wide social circle and a family that is supportive. Mrs Charles is now finding some of her caring role much more difficult: she gets very tired and irritable. Social services provide good support and have said that her husband could go into a care home. Mrs Charles does not know what she wants really, but knows that she needs help, as well as her husband.

Questions

- What type of help might be useful to Mrs Charles? From where could she get this?
- Who should provide help for carers in such a situation?
- Is help to Mrs Charles just going to delay a decision about her husband's care?
- Is it up to her family to sort this out?

Discussion on vignette 1 – Mrs Evans

Participants identified that a single, consistent contact person would be useful for Mrs Evans, and suggested that this might be found in or through the local Alzheimer's Society. They considered that Mrs Evans was not yet 'bad enough' for social services. Opinion was fairly split between those who believed that Mrs Evans should pay for the help she needed and that we should avoid a 'nanny State', and those who argued that the State should pay, because 'she had paid enough in council tax'. While the voluntary sector was seen as potentially useful for people such as Mrs Evans, it was recognised that creating a caring community was not easy.

Discussion on vignette 2 – Mr Gardner

This vignette was challenging, as Mr Gardner's circumstances seemed complex with no easy route to resolution. People recognised that he might be referred to social services but were not clear about what they could offer, and considered that they were in any event 'stretched to the limit'. Suggestions were made about him finding someone to talk to or ways in which he could reduce his isolation, such as by joining a club or church, but it was recognised that this was not easy. 'There should be a system', said one person, 'for people living on their own to be contacted and that should be a natural thing'. In many ways this illustration served to flag up again the idea that older people needed to have a form of regular visiting and, while some saw this as potentially helpful, others thought it impractical or controlling. So, while one person suggested the value of a local council keeping a list or register of people living alone, another observed that 'if you put people's names forward to be on it they get very offended'. Another put it bluntly, 'Well, if I was in this situation and I was depressed and stuff like that and someone tried to come in my flat, I'll tell them to bugger off'. Suggestions were made about the potential roles of residents' associations, of local churches, of community policing. For some, these overtures to Mr Gardner might work; others suggested that it might be that he would accept help only after a crisis when his needs were acute, such as facing eviction or being the victim of crime.

Discussion on vignette 3 – Mrs Charles

Interestingly, in this instance, many in the groups were quick to argue that Mrs Charles did not need just a small amount of help but rather a more extensive set of services, such as short-break or respite care. This could be a stay out of the house to give Mrs Charles a holiday or by Mr Charles attending day centre care. Some suggested that Mr Charles really needed full-time care, although his wife might feel guilty and might miss his company. All were agreed that she needed information: 'she needs an advice centre, in the town centre, in a shop, to give advice or obtain advice on everything'. Possibly drawing on personal experiences, one person suggested that there should be a single form or booklet for all applications and so on. Social services were generally agreed to be the source of help here, although one person did recognise that, for people like Mr and Mrs Charles, having good neighbours would be a real boon. 'You can have very, very, very good neighbours, but you really shouldn't expect them'. One person who had been looking after her disabled parent spoke of the difficulty of taking on the caring role:

> Going into the caring situation you don't know what's available and my father didn't want to have anything to do with social services ... I was looking after him for ten years.

Asked what should have been provided, she said: 'I don't know because you don't know where to go and you just plod on from day to day'.

Many in the groups were adamant that they did not believe that family should have to take on responsibility for supporting older people, although, as was evident in the paragraph above, many had taken on caring roles or were well supported by family. Two themes emerged, first that family members have other preoccupations: 'If your family's grown up they have their own problems'. Second, reliance on family can place a burden on them and alter the basis of the relationship: 'You can't make slaves of your family'. However, there were some who did see that family had responsibility and that this should be the role of the whole family, not just the one carer. It was up to the family to meet together to devise a 'collective solution'. One person said that the family should share responsibility if they could and, if they were able to help with the cost (of support), then they should.

Participants expressed a wish for someone to check up on people, to make sure they were all right. In the case of Mrs Charles, this was seen to be a suitable role for a health professional, but individuals were unclear about whether this would happen.

Appendix 2: Examples of 'preventative' services

All 15 authorities have some low-level preventative services or initiatives:

- housework and gardening directories and services
- handyman service
- warm and well service
- welfare rights advice
- community-based activities for adults and older people
- care networks
- cleaning, shopping, laundry and home maintenance
- care and repair
- carers' services
- fenland home age project and healthy homes partnership
- visiting schemes, befriending and telephone befriending
- Bangladeshi and African Caribbean befrienders
- services to individuals with Alzheimer's and their carers
- lunch and leisure clubs
- welcome home from hospital schemes
- home safety checks with the fire service
- campaigns on bogus callers with police and home care services

- community transport
- active ageing events including exercise, t'ai chi, walking and singing groups
- gentle exercise scheme
- assistive technology including telecare
- extra care housing
- mobile wardens, floating wardens and navigator roles
- localised independent living centres
- multi-functional resource centres
- link age networks
- independent benefit advice
- independence advisers
- age concern wellcheck and supporting you
- housework brokers' scheme
- partnership club including register
- partnership club *About Life* magazine
- memory catcher project.

  (McTigue, 2005, para. 8.1)